T0196227

THE GOD OF ELIJAH

My Encounter with the Supernatural Healing Power of God

Cheryl Simone

authorHOUSE®

AuthorHouse™
1663 Liberty Drive
Bloomington, IN 47403
www.authorhouse.com
Phone: 1-800-839-8640

First published by AuthorHouse 11/30/2011

ISBN: 978-1-4634-3165-5 (e)
ISBN: 978-1-4634-3166-2 (hc)
ISBN: 978-1-4634-3167-9 (sc)

Library of Congress Control Number: 2011911687

Printed in the United States of America

Any people depicted in stock imagery provided by Thinkstock are models,
and such images are being used for illustrative purposes only.
Certain stock imagery © Thinkstock.

This book is printed on acid-free paper.

Because of the dynamic nature of the Internet, any web addresses or links contained in
this book may have changed since publication and may no longer be valid. The views
expressed in this work are solely those of the author and do not necessarily reflect the
views of the publisher, and the publisher hereby disclaims any responsibility for them.

Watching my sister slip away into an eternal place and hearing the gratification in her voice as she transformed to the other side is what gives me peace. We walked together in that tunnel. I can't help but wonder what if I would have remained there too. Would I have experienced the same overwhelming joy my sister felt, instead of letting the paralyzing fear take over me causing me to be left behind?

What I experienced would make any individual wish that they were dead. Still I continue to hear how blessed I am to be alive. If I knew what I would be faced with when I awakened, I wonder if I would have rather remained asleep...

I stopped trying to figure out why I survived and have learned to embrace the encounter I had with The God of Elijah. If you have picked up this book, The God of Elijah desires to have an encounter with you. Jesus said that no man comes to Him, except God draws them. So relax, quiet your soul, and come with me on my journey, as I reveal what happens when the miraculous shows up.

Death stared me in the face; Hell was hard on my heels. Up against it, I didn't know which way to turn; then I called out to GOD for help: "Please, GOD!" I cried out. "Save my life!" GOD is gracious it is He who makes things right, our most compassionate God. GOD takes the side of the helpless; when I was at the end of my rope, He saved me. I said to myself, "Relax and rest. GOD has showered you with blessings. Soul, you've been rescued from death; Eye, you've been rescued from tears; and you, Foot, were kept from stumbling (MSG) Psalm 116: 3-8

Biography

*C*heryl Simone, a native of Trenton, New Jersey, is a multi-talented writer of original songs, poetry and short stories. She began writing at a very young age. Cheryl enjoys writing stories from her soul that releases emotions everyone can relate to. She is the daughter of Thomas L. and Vera M. Brown, and mother of two extraordinary children, Jawane and Jazzmen Hooper. In her free time she enjoys traveling and ministering to people whose souls are hanging in the balance.

Dedication

This book is dedicated to my parents, Mr. Thomas L. and Vera M. Brown, and my precious children Jawane Kalaif and Jazzmen Khadajah Hooper. You have filled my life with joy and continue to be my strength to go on. I love you with all of my heart.

Contents

Foreword

I count it both a privilege and pleasure to do this Foreword for my dear friend Cheryl. When I met Cheryl, we were co-workers. But over the past 20 plus years, we've become family.

I believe that God by His sovereign will allowed Cheryl to go through the experiences that are written of in this wonderful book. I also believe that God will use her story to increase someone's faith and trust in Him. Throughout this book those who already believe God to be who He is will no doubt keep on believing while those who aren't believers will begin to believe God to be who He says He is.

There are two main points of interest you will see about God when you read this book:

1. You will see that He is the God that healeth (Jehovah-Rapha).
2. You will see that He is the God who provides (Jehovah-Jireh).

God both healed and provided for Cheryl throughout this whole experience. Life has a way of propelling us into situations that we never imagined being in – Chapter 6 – The Journey. A lot of times, we look at situations, scenarios, predicaments and circumstances and say 'I could never go through this or make it through that', but through hindsight we see that the God we serve can and is capable of bringing us through any and everything. We must keep hold of the knowledge that we are going through. We're not in it to stay.

Let's focus on the word 'through' for a minute. Through speaks of something beginning but having an end. So again, whatever we go through in this life, there will be an end to it. Life itself is a going through process. The indication is that life as we know it will one day come to an end. The thing that we need to remind ourselves of is that if we trust in God's abilities, He'll bring whatever it is we're going through to an end.

Psalm 23:4 "Yea, though I walk through the valley of the shadow of death, I will fear n evil: for thou are with me; thy rod and thy staff they comfort me." You will see that Cheryl literally went through the valley of the shadow of death. Note the words in this passage, death was only a shadow and a shadow is not the actual or reality of what is represents. Your shadow is not you. It is only a silhouette. Sometimes death will only show you its' shadow, and we become fearful of something that's on a shadow. Notice that the Scripture goes on to say that we should not fear. The reason why we don't fear is because of the assurance that God is with us. God showed Cheryl that He was with her throughout this event that took place in her life.

Isaiah 43:2 "When thou passest through the waters, I will be with thee; and through the rivers, they shall not overflow thee; when thou walkest through the fire, thou shalt not be burned." The word through is used three times in this passage, which further establishes this point. Life consists of "going through". The thing about going through is that we don't always have the convenience of choosing what we go through and how we go through. Someone once said that God never promised us a smooth ride, but we are assured of a safe landing. After reading this powerful testimony, you will see that Cheryl went through a rough ride but she landed safely.

My prayer for everyone who reads this book is that you will see the awesomeness of our God.

The Very Reverend Curtis J. Cohen
Founder-Chief Pastor
Cush Worship & Deliverance Temple, Inc.

Introduction

For I consider that the sufferings of this present time are not worthy to be compared with the glory which shall be revealed in us. (NKJV) Romans 8:18

We may not always understand why things happen. However, in the core of every situation is a greater glory waiting to be revealed. Life is full of tests and trials. No one is exempt from going through challenging situations. The Word of God tells us that Man born of Woman is of few days, and full of trouble. Taking our eyes off of the situation and putting it on God will grant us the strength we need to endure. In the end, you will come out victorious with a greater understanding of what you have been anointed to do. Crisis provokes change; yet the willingness to adjust to that change will determine your growth. Although it never feels good to go through adversity, it births strength from within that you never knew existed.

I've spent countless hours trying to figure out why I survived, while others have expired from what appeared to be lesser. Wrestling with survivor's guilt deprived me of executing my gift and operating in the anointing that comes through having a relationship with God, or after being upon the bed of affliction. Regardless of how inauspicious your situation may appear, placing your trust in the God of Elijah will result in a miracle every single time. It is my prayer that as you turn the pages you will have an encounter with The God of Elijah. Flow with me, as I pour out waterfalls from within my soul.

Life would be incomplete without experiencing highs and lows. No matter where you are in life, "*The God of Elijah*" will refresh your faith in God, and minister to the depths of your soul. As you are reading this right now, *The God of Elijah* desires to have an encounter with you.

Chapter 1
Thy Will Be Done

After this manner therefore pray ye: Our Father which art in heaven, Hallowed be thy name. Thy kingdom come, Thy will be done in earth, as it is in heaven. Give us this day our daily bread. And forgive us our debts, as we forgive our debtors. And lead us not into temptation, but deliver us from evil: For thine is the kingdom, and the power, and the glory, for ever. Amen. (KJV) Matthew 6:9-13

When we pray this prayer, are we ready to accept God's will being done in our life, or are we only focusing on His provision, forgiveness and protection? What if His will meant someone being born blind? What if His will include a person leaving, or losing their job? What if His will was something similar to the biblical experience of Job? The disciples asked Jesus a question;

Now as Jesus passed by, He saw a man who was blind from birth. And His disciples asked Him, saying, "Rabbi, who sinned, this man or his parents, that he was born blind?" Jesus answered, "Neither this man nor his parents sinned, but that the works of God should be revealed in him."(NKJV) John 9:1-3

What if His will meant today you had to let go of a loved one? If so would you despise the will of God or would you respond like King David when his child with Bathsheba died? Would you respond like Job when he lost everything or his wife who encouraged him to curse God and die? What would your response be?

David therefore pleaded with God for the child and David fasted and went in and lay all night on the ground. So the elders of his house arose and went to him, to raise him up from the ground. But he would not, nor did he eat food with them. Then on the seventh day it came to pass that the child died. And the servants of David were afraid to tell him that the child was dead. For they said, "Indeed, while the child was alive, we spoke to him, and he would not heed our voice how can we tell him that the child is dead? He may do some harm!" When David saw that his servants were whispering, David perceived that the child was dead.

Therefore David said to his servants, "Is the child dead?" And they said, "He is dead." So David arose from the ground, washed and anointed himself and changed his clothes; and he went into the house of the LORD and worshiped Then he went to his own house; and when he requested, they set food before him, and he ate (NKJV) 2 Samuel 12:16-20

Then his wife said to him, "Do you still hold fast to your integrity? Curse God and die!"

But he said to her, "You speak as one of the foolish women speaks. Shall we indeed accept good from God, and shall we not accept adversity?" In all this Job did not sin with his lips. (NKJV) Job 2:9-10

Many of us want only the blessings without going through trials and tribulations. Sometimes we will be thrust into a situation just so God can show us what He can bring us out of. The bible records in Matthew 5:45, "He causes his sun to rise on the evil and the good, and sends rain on the righteous and the unrighteous." His will at times may leave you stunned and asking the question, "Lord why me?", yet through it all, God extends His grace to help us get through.

And He said to me, "My grace is sufficient for you, for My strength is made perfect in weakness." Therefore most gladly I will rather boast in my infirmities, that the power of Christ may rest upon me (NKJV) 2 Corinthians 12:9

It doesn't matter who you are, you are going to be confronted with adversity and challenges in this life. How you see God, determines your outcome and your growth. Adjusting to change is not easy, but it is inevitable. When we swathe our minds around the Word of God, our most difficult situation becomes bearable. Suffering is something we cannot avoid and certainly never become comfortable with. Women never get use to labor pains regardless of how many births, cancer patients never get use to the sickly feeling from chemo therapy, and humans never get use to a nagging toothache. With each incident there is a new level of pain to conquer each time. My deepest pain has not come from a broken bone, major surgery, or during child birth delivery. Although those experiences are very painful physically, my deepest pain has stemmed emotionally from being robbed of the opportunity to say goodbye to a loved one. In the past, I have taken the word "goodbye" for granted. I never contemplated that the word "goodbye" would be the final salutation as we parted. Just as I have taken the Lord's Prayer lightly concerning God's Will being done when there were tragic circumstances. Instead, I have found myself saying, "No, it can't be!", but if it's God's Will then it shall be done. This is what the Word of God instructs us to say concerning His Will;

Whereas you do not know what will happen tomorrow. For what is your life? It is even a vapor that appears for a little time and then vanishes away. Instead you ought to say, "If the Lord wills, we shall live and do this or that. (NKJV) James 4:14-15

On that particular morning when I prayed that prayer, I wasn't ready for His will to unfold in my life as it did. As I crawled into the backseat of my SUV to nap, nothing could have prepared me for the arduous journey ahead. When I awakened from my rest fourteen days later, my sister was gone. The last time I saw her was on a Sunday morning. The sun was shining brightly outside, but the presence of her aura was strong and radiant like the rays of the sun as she completed the final day of a forty day fast. I imagine the same glory that rested upon Moses on Mount Sinai was upon her, as she sat peacefully typing away on the keyboard.

Now the glory of the LORD rested on Mount Sinai, and the cloud covered it six days. And on the seventh day He called to Moses out of the midst of the cloud. The sight of the glory of the LORD was like a consuming fire on the top of the mountain in the eyes of the children of Israel. So Moses went into the midst of the cloud and went up into the mountain. And Moses was on the mountain forty days and forty nights. (NKJV) Exodus 24:16-18

The ambiance was calming and peaceful as I watched her from across the room. I saw her physical body before my eyes, but it was like I could see through her at the same time. Not a word was spoken. It felt like the presence of God showed up and we were still. Whatever was taking place was happening right before our eyes, but we couldn't see it. To the natural eye, it looked as if she was deep in thought, but she was somewhere between heaven and earth. Something appeared different about her that morning, and in all of the years I had known her that day was mysteriously unique. Standing near her, I possessed an eerie feeling. As I walked by, a strong presence engulfed her like a force field was protecting her from any contamination. It was unusual. As she approached the door, she turned around and said, "Sophia, take care of Ashley, goodbye Wayne." Before departing Georgia we prayed in the driveway…

"Our Father which art in heaven, Hallowed be thy name. Thy kingdom come, Thy will be done in earth, as it is in heaven"…

I climbed in the backseat to sleep as my sister Artisse (Arty) sat quietly in the front passenger seat and our brother Thomas (T.C.) drove off.

To everything there is a season, A time for every purpose under heaven: A time to be born, And a time to die; A time to plant, And a time to pluck what is planted; A time to kill, And a time to heal; A time to break down, And a time to build up; A time to weep, And a time to laugh; A time to mourn, And a time to dance; A time to cast away stones, And a time to gather stones; A time to embrace, And a time to refrain from embracing; A time to gain, And a time to lose; A time to keep, And a time to throw away; A time to tear, And a time to sew; A time to keep silence, And a time to speak; (NKJV) Ecclesiastes 3:1-8

Chapter 2
Sunday Morning

"Father, if it is Your will, take this cup away from Me; nevertheless not My will, but Yours be done." (NKJV) Luke 22:42

*O*h my God, I'm flying! I saw the traffic flow beneath me. As I projected toward the heavens everything suddenly halted, and my body began to spiral downward. I saw traffic moving along, I thought to myself, "Cheryl land on your feet, land on your feet." My stomach dropped, I could feel a divine assistance interrupting the fall. The angel cuffed me beneath my arm pits, and graciously rested my broken, bruised and battered body onto Interstate 85.

For He shall give His angels charge over you, To keep you in all your ways. In their hands they shall bear you up, Lest you dash your foot against a stone. (NKJV) Psalm 91:11, 12

As my gold Mercury Mountaineer came to an abrupt halt, and faced on coming traffic my brother sat in disbelief as he reflected on what had just transpired. He struggled to remember the number of times the SUV rolled over, as he gripped the steering wheel for dear life. The scenario played like a motion picture in his mind. Moments before the accident he recalled hearing me mumble in my sleep, "T.C. look out"... My body was still in one piece stretched out along the back seat of my vehicle as I attempted to catch a nap. A quick glance suggested to my siblings that I was asleep, and they both giggled at the fact that I was talking in my sleep. The urge to tell me to put on my seat belt made an impression in his mind. Cognizance of the warning, yet he resisted the unction to follow his gut feeling as he continued driving. Meanwhile, I dreamt that a truck was running us off the road. T.C. recalls the tone of the moments prior to the accident reflecting the calming and peaceful feeling that was felt back at Arty's home earlier that morning. Everything happened suddenly, a smaller car jetted out in front of our vehicle leaving no time to brake, he lost control. The car responsible for the accident kept going while our SUV fishtailed out of control, before it violently careened multiple times across the highway; and that quickly the first stage of the tragedy ceased, as the SUV rested on flattened wheels facing oncoming traffic.

Involuntary anguish and chills penetrated his being, as he glanced over to see Arty's flesh separated from her skull. Instantly he knew she was gone. In a very faint voice he mumbled, "Cheryl, you alright? Cheryl?" As he turned around there was no sign of me in the vehicle. Fear and shock exploded throughout his body. The screeching cars facing head-on and spectators running toward him played out in slow motion. Abrupt fear paralyzed him momentarily until adrenaline kicked in jolting him back into the reality of the moment. After bidding farewell to his older sister, he exits the salvaged truck only to collapse to the ground with a broken leg. He observed me in the distance trapped perilously between cars and desperately he painfully scooted over to me as I lay one with the concrete.

In the twinkling of an eye I experienced the following vision as I was surrounded by an illuminating light. Everything around me became oblivious in the bright light: Arty and I were walking in a tunnel full of light. My sister kept waving to me to come on, the more I walked the brighter it became. Mere words cannot explain the brightness of the lights, or the tranquility of the serene presence that surrounded us in the tunnel. I felt a very light feeling like I was gliding or being drawn by a force. I imagine it's what it would feel like to be floating between clouds.

The light was the brightest I had ever seen. It gave the blinding effect of staring into the sun for too long. My sister kept saying, "Cheryl this is beautiful, you've got to see this, come on." I continued walking in the tunnel and the more I walked the brighter it became. Arty began to disappear ahead as if she was slipping away into another place. Her voice became faint almost to a whisper as she uttered, "Oh my goodness, this is beautiful, Cheryl you have got to see this, come on." I was frightened by the intensity of the light and hesitancy forced me not to move forward. I turned around and began to run out like a panting deer away from the light. As I looked back to see what had become of my sister the vision faded."

My body which had seen better days lay impaired on the asphalt and the angel disappeared into space. Within seconds I was observed attempting to raise myself up from off the ground. At that moment I was unaware that my upper torso was the only body part still intact. Vaguely I heard shouts of "Don't move her," ringing out as my brother made an attempt to drag me to safety. The shouts intensified, "Don't move her! Don't move her!" the shouts penetrated the airways, as the spectators awaited for paramedics to arrive. Police later reported from witnesses on the scene that my SUV rolled over five times before my body was ejected, and thrown into the air like a rag doll. I was thrown thirty feet across, and projected as high as the highway lamp post. While the turbulence around me unfolded, I laid in a trap on the concrete road between time and eternity.

And in a window sat a certain young man named Eutychus, who was sinking into a deep sleep. He was overcome by sleep; and as Paul continued speaking, he fell down from the third story, and was taken up dead. But Paul went down, fell on him, and embracing him said, "Do not trouble yourselves; for his life is in him." (NKJV) Acts 20:9,10

T.C. and I had departed New Jersey on February 1st, 2003 around 11:00a.m.. Our original plans were to leave by 8:00 a.m., but I spent the previous night galloping in Atlantic City until the wee hours of the morning. Desperate for a nap, I stretched out in the comfort of my own bed to rest. Strangely that morning I dreamt of a school bus running a car off of the road. A loud pounding on the door awakened me; "Cheryl! It's after 10:00a.m.. I've been calling you for the past two hours" T.C. exclaimed. I sprung up, showered and threw a change of clothes into a backpack. By 11:00a.m. we were moving along the New Jersey Turnpike heading to Dahlonega, Georgia. Two days earlier the family received the news about Marlins fatal heart attack. He was a friend of the family. His wife Connie and Arty were best friends since childhood. They were close like sisters so Arty wanted to be there for her, by giving support and showing love during her time of bereavement.

She was unable to get a flight out in a reasonable time, so T.C. and I made the decision to go and pick her up. It was about 1:00 a.m. on February 2, 2003, as we pulled into Arty's driveway. A little catching up took place between us before settling down. It was almost 2:00 a.m. when Arty placed a call to our sister Robin who resided in Charlotte, North Carolina. She left the following message, *"Robin, Cheryl and T.C. arrived safe. We will be leaving in the morning to pick you up. I'll call you when we get close, goodnight."* *click*

I was exhausted from the long drive to Georgia and very tired from the all night escapade in Atlantic City the night before. We all went to bed for a few hours in order to prepare to reverse our route that morning. It had been several months since I last saw her and I managed to spend our last hours together asleep. I took for granted that we would have more time to fulfill the simple things in life. My mind wonders what we would have talked about. What exactly do you say to a person if you know it's your last time together? Would I have told her that I loved her and that I was sorry for all of our childhood fights or that I admired how she was always pleasant and saw the good in everyone? When Arty met a person she understood that they were a spirit made in the image of God. She didn't see their skin tone or judge them on their social economic background. She was respectful to every individual she came into contact with even if they were harsh toward her. Rarely did I ever hear her raising her voice.

A soft answer turns away wrath, but a harsh word stirs up anger. (NKJV) Proverbs 15:1

She remained composed and unruffled even in the midst of chaos, but I was the complete opposite.

Instead of conversing with her and sharing my heart I slept away our last moments together. I know I will see her again in eternity, but on holidays, birthdays, and special occasions, my heart aches at the absence of her presence. The last thing I remember hearing her say was The Lords Prayer. T.C. recalled a strange feeling that something was about to happen at the same time the urge came to him to awaken me to buckle up. Arty was quiet as if in a trance gazing ahead. No one spoke a word.

Then I heard a voice from heaven saying to me, "Write: 'Blessed are the dead who die in the Lord from now on.'" "Yes," says the Spirit, "that they may rest from their labors, and their works follow them." (NKJV) Revelations 14:13

Chapter 3
Resuscitate Her!

At Joppa there was a certain disciple named Tabitha, which is translated Dorcas. This woman was full of good works and charitable deeds which she did. But it happened in those days that she became sick and died. When they had washed her, they laid her in an upper room. And since Lydda was near Joppa, and the disciples had heard that Peter was there, they sent two men to him, imploring him not to delay in coming to them. Then Peter arose and went with them. When he had come, they brought him to the upper room. And all the widows stood by him weeping, showing the tunics and garments which Dorcas had made while she was with them. But Peter put them all out, and knelt down and prayed. And turning to the body he said, "Tabitha,

arise." And she opened her eyes, and when she saw Peter she sat up. Then he gave her his hand and lifted her up; and when he had called the saints and widows, he presented her alive. And it became known throughout all Joppa, and many believed on the Lord. (NKJV) Acts 9:36-42

Scene of Accident

*P*aramedics arrived on the scene after maneuvering through miles of gridlocked traffic. Bodies out of vehicles would suggest that chances for survivors were slim to none. In our case the fatality remained incubated between the dented steel that took on the appearance of a crushed aluminum can. One glance of observation for life revealed what the naked eye would witness without words. Arty was gone... to a better place.

The accident scene was chaotic as Paramedics desperately tried to intubate me with an endotracheal tube as medication was quickly pumped into my veins. My blood pressure rapidly took on the rate of a newborn baby decreasing by the second while more than two pints of my own blood supply trickled out. Restless attempts to get the tube in combined with the multiple trauma announced that time was running out. They were losing me! The blood loss and decline in pressure caused a temporary lose of consciousness, yet paramedics diligently worked to intubate my deflated lungs that were collapsed. My pressure continued to decline as blood loss increased by the second. Meanwhile, my dormant body rested in the hands of EMT professionals and my spirit in the hands of God. I slipped into total unconsciousness as my pressure dropped and pints of blood poured out of my open wounds. After many failed attempts, Paramedics ceased working and began to call into Greenville Memorial Hospital. Enroute with BF (black female) involved in MVA (motor vehicle accident), airway closed, low pressure, faint pulse, collapsed lungs, multiple trauma in the lower extremity, and head injuries.

My vision returned again. I saw the bright light. This time I yelled out for my sister, Arty! Arty! As I moved forward to find her the brightness dimmed, and began to slowly fade away. I stopped and stood still, waiting for her to return to me. As I inched forward the light began to disappear, I watched the light leave like a door was being shut.

Meanwhile the turbulence around me continued to

unfold as my spirit collided with death and my will to live battled to win the struggle.

Death stared me in the face; Hell was hard on my heels. Up against it, I didn't know which way to turn; then I called out to GOD for help: "Please, GOD!" I cried out. "Save my life!" GOD is gracious it is He who makes things right, our most compassionate God. GOD takes the side of the helpless; when I was at the end of my rope, He saved me. I said to myself, "Relax and rest. GOD has showered you with blessings. Soul, you've been rescued from death; Eye, you've been rescued from tears; and you, Foot, were kept from stumbling."(MSG) Psalm 116: 3-8

My body was placed on a gurney for transport as the sheet was being pulled up. One of my arms dangled off the side of the stretcher. Suddenly I lifted my arm and placed it across my chest. Immediately paramedics frantically made every attempt to resuscitate me as screams and cries bellowed out from on lookers, "She moved her arm! She's alive!" Work recommenced until a successful attempt to get the tube down in my larynx occurred. Within seconds what appeared to be hopeless was miraculously resurrected as constant pumps of an artificial breathing device shined light on a dark situation. The hospital was less than seven miles away and my critical state gave not a minute to spare. We rode in separate Ambulance as sirens warned traffic ahead that Sunday's midday flow was interrupted by our dreadful incident. Our arrival at Greenville Memorial Hospital turned February 2nd into a bizarre disturbing scene as our blood saturated bodies were whisked through the hallways. My 155lb body frame had taken on another appearance that would last for weeks. Arty's lifeless body was removed from the demolished vehicle and taken to the hospitals morgue.

Salvage crews were cleaning up the wreckage from the accident off of Interstate 85 which resonated of bone fragments, blood stains and death. Local miser's followed the tow truck to the salvage yard in an attempt to personate family members in order to retrieve personal property and handbags.

Back at the Emergency Room, a team of Doctors began cutting off what remained of my clothes only to view multiple open wound fractures, cuts, bruises, scrapes, skin lost, and edema. As prodigious damage lied beneath what the naked eye could see. On the other side of the partition in the Emergency room T.C.'s voice interrupted the examination as he asked, "Is she okay, what did she say?" Sir she's sedated please let us work, the doctor replied. I heard her; "Cheryl, can you hear me?" were the last words he uttered before the pain medication kicked in causing him to drift off into a state of sedation. After a Computed Tomography (CT) scan I was rushed into emergency surgery to undergo exploratory laparoscopy due to significant fluid in my abdomen and pelvis. My intubated body lost nearly 200 cc's of blood as doctors worked the next seven hours to perform numerous procedures. Several facial lacerations and a deep forehead gash closed with sutures and stained of dried blood was the least of the many life threatening injuries that I sustained. Both lungs were collapsed resulting in me being hooked up to a respirator. I also had a pelvis fracture that tore through my bladder and reproductive organ. Every bone below my pelvis except the femur was fractured significantly. I fractured my coccyx and I suffered a lower back and pancreas injury. The impact of the trauma caused major damage. A rupture spleen and possible liver laceration were amongst the list of injuries that complicated matters all the more. Ligaments, nerves, and joints were intertwined and unrecognizable as my badly mangled right foot dangled in the opposite direction hanging on by a thread.

On February 2nd that was the first day of one of eight surgeries to be performed at Greenville Memorial Hospital within a sixty-six day span.

For the Father loves the Son, and shows Him all things that He Himself does; and He will show Him greater works than these, that you may marvel. For as the Father raises the dead and gives life to them, even so the Son gives life to whom He will. (NKJV) John 5:20, 21

Little Star in my Eye

You were a gift, lent from above

So precious so sweet, so easy to love

God's love for you was so much more

I watched angels escort you into heavens door

I know it's the place you were meant to be

Sophia's doing a great job taking care of Ashley

My work here is still undone

You continued on, as I turned to run

Although your gone, a light still shines

In the broken hearts of those you left behind

I'm sad you're gone, but happy you're free

Don't forget to save a mansion for me

Next trip, I'll see you in eternity. – Cheryl S.

Chapter 4
The Tragic News

And there came a messenger unto Job, and said, The oxen were plowing and the asses feeding beside them: And the Sabeans fell upon them and took them away; yea, they have slain the servants with the edge of the sword; and I only am escaped alone to tell thee. While he was yet speaking there came also another, and said, The fire of God is fallen from heaven and hath burned up the sheep and the servants and consumed them; and I only am escaped alone to tell thee. While he was yet speaking, there came also another, and said, The Chaldeans made out three bands and fell upon the camels and have carried them away, yea, and slain the servants with the edge of the sword; and I only am escaped alone to tell thee. While he was yet

speaking, there came also another, and said, Thy sons and thy daughters were eating and drinking wine in their eldest brother's house: And behold, there came a great wind from the wilderness and smote the four corners of the house and it fell upon the young men and they are dead; and I only am escaped alone to tell thee. Then Job arose, and rent his mantle, and shaved his head, and fell down upon the ground, and worshipped, And said, Naked came I out of my mother's womb, and naked shall I return thither: the LORD gave, and the LORD hath taken away; blessed be the name of the LORD. (NKJV) Job 1:14-21

*A*fter T.C. was treated and discharged from the hospital with a broken leg, he was able to muster up enough strength to make the call bearing the tragic news to his wife. The tragedy released a shockwave throughout the family as our sister Robin patiently awaited our arrival in Charlotte, North Carolina unaware of what had taken place.

Mom and our sister Christine (Pie) were in church service that morning. Pie later describes that day as one she'll never forget. She spent the morning ushering to and fro, seat after seat, while the saints clapped their hands and patted their feet. Pastor JoAnn Wilson rose to preach the gospel; and within minutes into the sermon, T.C.'s wife Sabrina and daughter Karizma approached the church door. Pie had taken a seat in the back of the church near Barbara Johnson. Sister Johnson was the first to observe them before nudging Pie of their presence. She anxiously exited the sanctuary to see why her sister in law and niece were there. She could hear Karizma's voice tremble as she shared the unfortunate news with her, "Aunt Pie, my dad, Aunt Cheryl and Aunt Arty were in a car accident, and Aunt Arty was killed, and the doctors said Aunt Cheryl may not make it through the night." For whatever reason the information Karizma shared did not register right away. Pie responded the best she knew how, "Where is everyone at?" Suddenly the news became clear to her as she broke down crying and balling from the inside out. Karizma and Sabrina departed troubled and upset. Pie re-entered the church weeping and wondering what to do next. Barbara Johnson observed her state of distress and immediately helped her outside to the atrium area. Pie shared the news with Barbara who instantaneously pulled Deacon Donaldson to remain by her side. After investigating the reason for Pie's distraught state,

Barbara rushed inside the sanctuary to get our mother who was listening to the Word of God as it came forth with conviction. They stepped outside the church, as Pie shared the news with her. "Mom, Karizma just left, she told me Arty, Cheryl and T.C. were in a car accident. Cheryl is in critical condition and Arty was killed". Without hesitation she fainted and was soon helped to her feet and taken to the pastor's office to revive. Mom lamented heavily giving the impression that she was going to pass out again. The pain was intense and it provoked her to petition the Lord to take her instead. Between sobs she repeatedly mumbled "My Arty is gone, My Arty is dead."

Mom picked up the phone to call her Aunt Myrtle and all she could get out is, "Arty is gone Myrtle, my Arty is dead". Myrtle's scream echoed throughout the phone as mom held the receiver. Once she hung up and regained her composure, she was driven across town to be with Dad.

For the Lord will not cast off forever. Though He causes grief, Yet He will show compassion according to the multitude of His mercies. For He does not afflict willingly, Nor grieve the children of men. (NKJV) Lamentations 3:31-33

Back in Greenville, South Carolina at the hospital T.C. sat in a wheelchair as pain passed throughout his body. Dad mimicked the same posture at home in Trenton, New Jersey when he received the news. He collapsed down upon the couch and allowed salty tears to stream down his cheeks. He was speechless and continued to remain in that position motionlessly for several minutes. One arm rested across his chest as it met the arm that touched his face. His pain in that moment reminded him of the day he lost his mother suddenly to an asthma attack. Only this time the agony was greater as he experienced the loss of a child a nightmare no parent desires to go through. He shook his head in disbelief continuously and exhaled before stating, "Some day's life really hands it to you."

As Robin awaited our arrival in Charlotte, she paced the floors nervously, and spoke aloud in a puzzled voice, "Where are they?" She kept watching the clock as she sat at the kitchen table like a child anxiously waiting for the rain to stop to go outside and play. Before her nerves got the best of her she contacted Wayne, Arty's husband to confirm the time of our departure earlier that morning. Wayne responded based on the facts from earlier that day. Within minutes of hanging up the phone with Robin his phone rang again as his mother in law revealed the tragedy to him. The news about the accident caused him to nearly lose his mind. No number of years of serving as a Sergeant in the military could have prepared him to cope with the heartbreaking news he heard. Wayne and the girls were at home in Georgia when the call came in. Within minutes they dashed out the door wearing bedroom slippers on their feet as the car pulled out of the driveway. Life didn't warn them of the journey ahead as they crossed over into the state that had claimed the life of their wife and mother. Ashley sat quietly in the backseat in disbelief and confused. The melancholy expression on her face spoke volumes that words could not explain. She was torn between mixed emotions as she tried to understand what happened to her mother, and cope with the pain of losing her. Sophia the elder of the two cried uncontrollably as the pain of separation ripped her heart. The very thought of losing her mother sent her emotions on a course that continued to crash like tidal waves. Wayne tried to maintain his composure for the girl's sake while wrestling with the thought's of what had just come to pass. Robin continued to call our phones desperately trying to reach someone but she never got an answer. The original plan was to pick Arty up in Georgia and as we doubled back swing through and grab Robin who lived in Charlotte, at the time. Finally, Mom got in touch with Robin as she delivered this message; "Robin this is Mom, I need you to be calm and I need you to be strong, Arty, Cheryl and T.C were in an accident, and we lost Arty. I will call you back as soon as I hear more". *click* Robin was devastated. She screamed, cried, and yelled until her strength was gone. As Robin calmed herself down she recalled hearing Arty's voice on the other end of the phone earlier that day telling her that T.C. and I had safely arrived. Robin was distressed. Her dialogue with Arty on Saturday night replayed in her mind like a scratch record on a turntable. She thought how could this be I just spoke to her. Arty's calm voice continued to playback in her mind, *"Robin you're really going to need to be there for Connie, Marlin is gone and I need you to really be there for her because people are there when the person first dies, but once the funeral is over that's when the family needs help the most. Robin, God has given us all a glimpse of prophesy, He has revealed something to me. I have been on a forty day fast and I was going to break it today, but I need you to fast with me until 4 p.m. tomorrow. Don't eat anything and drink only water if you get hungry nibble on just a cracker. I'll give you a call when Cheryl and T.C. arrive."* The last time Robin heard Arty's voice she said, "*Cheryl and T.C. arrived safe*". Robin was very troubled as she tried to comprehend all that had transpired. The phone rang again. This time it was Pie calling to see if she was ok informing her that family members were on their way to comfort her. Robin hung up the phone with Pie, and contacted Janelle Barnett, a sister in Christ from Greater Salem Church, to share the misfortune with her. Janelle, Barbara and Mother McLeod, members of the church she attended arrived at her home within thirty minutes prepared to drive her to Greenville, South Carolina.

Time waited for no one. Several hours had passed and my children and their father Juan were still unaware of the situation. Mom called my job to leave an urgent message for my best friend Tammie Gooding to call her. Tammie received the message and returned Mom's call immediately. When mom answered the phone all Tammie heard on the other end was, "She's gone… She's gone"… Tammie exclaimed, "Vera! Who's gone?" Officer Troy Mickens overheard Tammie and released a scream loud enough to shatter glass as she stood nearby freaking out. Tammie petitioned Troy to calm down so that she could hear what my mother was saying. Every muscle in her body contracted as she asked in a soft whisper, "Vera, who's gone?" "Tell me what happened?" Mom replied, "Arty is gone, my firstborn, she's gone." A slight sigh of relief came over Tammie that she was not talking about me but an expression of sorrow hit her as she conversed with a mother who had just lost her firstborn child. Tammie sobbed as mom shared with her the report of my critical state and the slim chance of me surviving long enough for anyone to arrive. Tammie could not imagine the pain mom must have felt to learn that three of her children were in a terrible car wreck. Once she hung up the phone Tammie informed the Lieutenant on duty, Daniel Murray of the news she received. Lt. Murray excused himself to the privacy of a restroom to break down one teardrop at a time. Tammie was relieved of her duties in order to get herself together. As Tammie exited the building, she noticed a memo up announcing that I was in an accident. The memo listed every injury known at that time that I sustained. The sight of it sent her into a rage because never in the history of East Jersey State Prison was a memo so detailed. She tore it down and then proceeded to the main building to remove the memo that was posted over there. She contacted the Police Benevolent Association (PBA) representative and suggested it be replaced with fewer details. A new memo was reposted informing fellow co-workers that I was in a car accident, and nothing more.

During Tammie's hour and a half drive home she recalls nothing. Everything was a fog to her. There was barely any traffic on the New Jersey Turnpike and she doesn't recall how she even made it home. The news spread throughout the workplace faster than a missile. Some co-workers were driven to tears, yet remained hopeful in the midst of the uncouth ones that used it as an opportunity to create a gambling pool. Chances of my survival, versus my demise…

I shall not die, but live, and declare the works of the LORD. The LORD has chastened me severely; but He has not given me over to death. (NKJV) Psalm 118:17, 18

When Tammie arrived home she began to pray and talk to God. She recalls it being the most selfish prayer she ever prayed. She didn't quite know how to pray, so she just talked to the Lord like she was talking to another person. She simply asked God, "Please don't take her, we need her here. She is a counselor for some, a psychiatrist to others, and a dear friend to me, please don't take her now". The entire time she believed that I was going to pull through. After she felt a peace upon her that it was well, she contacted my mother and proceeded to Trenton to spend the rest of the evening with my family.

EAST JERSEY STATE PRISON IS SADDENED TO REPORT

SCO. CHERYL HOOPER HAS BEEN ADMITTED INTO THE ICU AT MEMORIAL HOSPITAL IN GREENVILLE, S.C. DUE TO A CAR ACCIDENT.

SHE IS HOSPITALIZED AT: MEMORIAL HOSPITAL GREENVILLE, S.C. PATIENT INFORMATION 1-864-455-7000

FURTHER INFORMATION WILL FOLLOW

My good friend Vincent Welch (Vinny) was in Atlantic City where I had left him the night before. We both shared a gambling addiction that was hard to kick. He was sitting at the blackjack table when his phone began to vibrate. He stepped away from the table to answer the call. Officer Andre Williams was on the other end to inform him that I had been in a car accident and was comatose. Right away he regretted not talking me out of the drive to Georgia because he had a bad feeling that something was going to go wrong. His assumption was that I had fallen asleep behind the wheel. Vinny immediately departed Atlantic City in tears as his mind recalled seeing me hours earlier. We were gambling together with my god daughter Melvina, cousin's Hazel and Rosey, and my neighbor Monk. As we departed he said, "Be careful and try to get some rest before you leave". He remembers my eyes being blood shot red and me being extremely tired.

Keith, the youngest sibling was away at school in Massachusetts when the accident occurred. Cousin Marcus tried to reach him by phone earlier that day, but there was no answer. Keith played on the basketball team for the college he was attending. He was away at a basketball game during the time Marcus called his phone. He didn't respond to the messages until he returned to his dormitory room around 11 p.m. . . He returned the call and Aunt Mae Baker picked up on the other end as she shared the tragic news with him. Keith sent the phone hurling across the room before he collapsed down upon the bed. He was stiff as his hands cuffed both sides of his head and the tears ran down his face like a waterfall. In that moment he felt the effect of losing his favorite sister as so many things began to cloud his mind. He remembered how she catered to him and wondered how mom and dad were holding up. Keith was concerned about how T.C. and I were doing. He thought about Wayne, Sophia and Ashley and how devastated they must have been. He needed answers. The next morning couldn't arrive fast enough for him to board the Amtrak train back to New Jersey. As his feet left the platform in Massachusetts, he never looked back.

Melvina, my goddaughter, was at home when she received the call that sent her into a frenzy. She cried until her head ached and her eyes were sore before contacting my first cousin Felicia Brown. The two of them decided to drive to Greenville, South Carolina the next morning unprepared for what they would witness the next day. In the meantime, Mom continued making calls to family, friends, and reservations to fly out to Greenville South Carolina.

It was approximately 8 p.m. on Sunday night when Robin arrived at the hospital. I was in emergency surgery while T.C. remained in the same position from earlier that day. Local parishioners were present in the I.C.U. waiting area to offer prayer and support in anyway they could. As Robin approached T.C, he was motionless. She greeted him with a hug to comfort him, and then kissed his forehead. Still he remained in a trance. Afterwards she proceeded to the Operating Room area but had no idea which Operating Room I was in. She asks the Holy Spirit to lead her to the correct doors that I was behind. Janelle, Barbara, and Mother McLeod stood aside praying as Robin laid her hands on the door and cried out to God. "If you are the God of Elijah, you will not let Cheryl die too. I speak life; she shall live and not die", as she prayed the Word of God.

"I shall not die, but live, And declare the works of the LORD." (NKJV) Psalm 118:17

"I call her back right now!" As she stood outside the Operating Room door praying the hospital shook like an aftershock from an earthquake. Robin continued to cry out to God, and He delivered me from the grips of death.

…God is our refuge and strength, A very present help in trouble. (NKJV) Psalm 46:1

See, I have inscribed you on the palms of My hands; Your walls are continually before Me. (NKJV) Isaiah 49:16

The entire floor trembled as Robin prayed to The God of Elijah for my healing. Hour's later doctors approached her in the waiting room with information regarding my condition. I was in a critical state, comatose on life support. The doctor stated that they had done all that they could do to make me comfortable, but I was not expected to make it throughout the night. I had suffered numerous broken bones and several internal injuries and if I survived my right leg may need to be amputated. After hearing that news Robin made her way to a narrow kitchen nearby where she created an altar and continued to cry out to The God of Elijah for a miracle.

Let us therefore come boldly to the throne of grace that we may obtain mercy and find grace to help in time of need. (NKJV)Hebrews 4:16

But He was wounded for our transgressions, He was bruised for our iniquities; The chastisement for our peace was upon Him, And by His stripes we are healed. (NKJV) Isaiah 53:5

It took nearly all day and night before mom was able to locate my ex-husband Juan. My children were with him in Jersey City, New Jersey enjoying the presence of their dad. It was 10 p.m. when Mom's persistence finally paid off as she smacked Juan with the news that changed my life forever.

After hearing the news he understood why I had not returned his calls about picking up the children. His heart raced wildly as he tried to figure out what to do next. Our children were watching television and playing with their cousins upstairs. He called his sister Diane downstairs to share the news with her first. She let out a loud scream that echoed throughout the house. It startled everyone and raised their curiosity at the same time. Her scream alerted everyone in the house that something was wrong. As the children slowly approached the staircase to see what was going on, Juan called both children downstairs and sat them down. Jazzmen sat on his lap and Jawane under one arm as he shared this with them; "Your Mom, Uncle T.C., and Aunt Arty were in a car accident. Your Aunt Arty was killed and your Mom is hurt really bad". The children started to cry right away and seeing their dad cry made them cry even harder. Juan's siblings tried to console them before he packed their bags and by midnight they were on the road heading to Greenville, South Carolina.

During the night, T.C's wife, and his sister's in law Sharon and Gail nervously arrived at the hospital. Shortly after their arrival Wayne, Sophia and Ashley showed up scared and anxious. It was early morning when mom's flight touched down in Greenville, South Carolina and she proceeded straight to the hospital charged up instead of checking into a hotel. When she arrived she witnessed me on life support, comatose with tubes everywhere. She counted the tubes going into different parts of my body, all eight of them, but not once did she doubt the Word of the Lord.

Who has believed our report? And to whom has the arm of the LORD been revealed? But He was wounded for our transgressions, He was bruised for our iniquities; The chastisement for our peace was upon Him, And by His stripes we are healed. (NKJV) Isaiah 53:1, 5

Blessed is she who believed, for there will be a fulfillment of those things which were told her from the Lord." (NKJV) Luke 1:45

On this side to the human eye it looked hopeless as if all was lost. Doctors worked diligently to return me to a place that man considers to be normal as my will to live struggled against mortality. Then a familiar voice whispered in my ear, "Look up and live doll, God said, look up and live"... MOM!!!

Chapter 5
Look up and Live

Then the LORD said to Moses, "Make a fiery serpent, and set it on a pole; and it shall be that everyone who is bitten, when he looks at it, shall live." So Moses made a bronze serpent, and put it on a pole; and so it was, if a serpent had bitten anyone, when he looked at the bronze serpent, he lived. (NKJV) Numbers 21:8, 9

My Mom came into the hospital room and bent down in my ear and began to speak to my soul. I heard her loud and clear. "Look up and live doll. God said, Look up and live". I heard her! Even in a comatose state I heard her calling me back from drifting to the other side. Tears streamed along side my face to let her know that although my physical mobility may have been quiescent, my spirit was alive and willing to respond. Family members often wonder if a loved one can hear them when they are in a coma. I say, "Yes they can!" Although unable to physically respond, I am a living testimony that your spirit will respond in its own way. Every time she whispered those words into my ears my spirit man leaped like a dolphin swimming in the ocean.

For the word of God is living and powerful, and sharper than any two-edged sword, piercing even to the division of soul and spirit, and of joints and marrow, and is a discerner of the thoughts and intents of the heart. (NKJV)Hebrew 4:12

Each time Mom approached my bedside she uttered these words, "Look up and live doll". God said, "Look up and live". While doctor's inputted their wisdom, skills and knowledge Mom with no medical degree simply spoke life.

"It is written, 'Man shall not live by bread alone, but by every word that proceeds from the mouth of God.'" (NKJV) Matthew 4:4

She spoke the Word of God, the missing component for my present situation.

It is the Spirit who gives life; the flesh profits nothing. The words that I speak to you are spirit, and they are life. (NKJV) John 6:63

Mom stood over me and cried like a little girl whose doll legs had popped off only her doll was not made of plastic but of fragments of her very being woven into another person. She was broken because a piece of her heart left with my sister Arty. The pain she felt was not all hers, but a portion of what she wanted to carry for me as I laid in that bed and still she had to be that shoulder for my other siblings to cry on. After mom came out of the room from speaking to my soul my brother requested to see me, T.C. was rolled into the I.C.U. to be by my bedside. T.C. thought he had the strength to weather my condition, but what he witnessed caused him to break down completely. His thoughts were raging like a violent storm, tormenting him. His tears flowed like torrential rain, yet nothing could blur the vision of seeing Arty's disfiguration in that car. It was too much, too soon. He was dealing with his own physical pain, the grief of losing a sister, and the threat of possibly losing another one. He tried to blame himself for a situation that was beyond man's control. In that moment he didn't see the brighter side, the storm pass on, and the sun shining again. He was in reality, and all of the components pierced his heart and bombarded his mind causing him to weep hysterically. When the family saw him come out, no one knew what to expect. Later that morning Juan arrived worried with our two children, Jawane and Jazzmen, who were afraid of hearing the outcome. T.C. encouraged Juan to see me without the children thinking it was going to be too much for them because it was definitely difficult enough for the adults. The family was concerned how the children would react. Wayne volunteered to go with him before the children were allowed in.

Juan couldn't believe that this was the same woman he laid eyes on 15 years ago. Lying before him was not the cute petite young lady he met at 19 years old with the big brown legs. This could not possibly be the woman whose hand he asked in marriage and bare him two beautiful talented children. What he witnessed was unsightly and ugly, but not unpleasant enough to keep the children away. Depriving them of seeing me would have been harder on them, and left them wondering why not. As he walked away no demon from our past would be strong enough to withdraw him from being by my side during that time. Divorced or not, he responded like a husband.

But from the beginning of the creation, God 'made them male and female 'For this reason a man shall leave his father and mother and be joined to his wife, and the two shall become one flesh'; so then they are no longer two, but one flesh. Therefore what God has joined together, let not man separate."
(NKJV) Mark 10:6-9

Juan escorted Jawane and Jazzmen into the area. They walked right pass me as they were unable to identify their own mother. As I lay motionless against life and death my body was swollen beyond recognition almost three times my normal size from the multiple traumas. They observed several machines connected to my body to keep me functioning. Jawane thought to himself, what are all these tubes and machines for? He didn't quite understand why there was a tube inserted into my throat area or metal and screws on my abdomen and leg. Jawane gently rubbed my swollen hand as he spoke, "Hi mommy, its Jawane, its going to be okay, I'm here, I love you mommy". His attention was redirected to the large gash on my forehead and he wondered why the dry blood was not cleaned away as he sighed. He then thought to himself *at least her hair is still the same*, but he couldn't help but focus on the external fixator's upon my body. His delicate mind tried to understand how a contraption that looked so painful was going to help me in anyway. He could not believe that a car accident had the ability to create such a drastic outcome. Jazzmen paid close attention to her brother's response. The identical issues captured her attention raising questions in her eight year old mind. She didn't understand the object that rested on my abdomen. She wondered *will mommy have to live with this the rest of her life.* She gently touched my other hand and called out, "Mom"…"Mom" before asking her dad, "Why isn't she answering me?" Juan told her that I was in a deep sleep and would not be able to talk with the tube in my throat. Jazzmen then asked her father if she could get in the bed with me. He told her that it was not a good idea to touch me at that time. The nurse entered the room and Jazzmen asked her if she was there to wash me up because I still had dried blood on me. Her next question to the nurse was, "Where is her pee-pee coming from?" Seeing me like that made her unhappy while she thought to herself, Uncle T.C. must feel really bad. He only has a broken leg. She wanted to see her Aunt Arty as she tried to imagine what happened to her if I looked like that. The bright side to her downside is that she was happy to be out of school.

Family members continued to arrive in Greenville. Cousin Beverly, Preston, Allen, Sandra and Kirby drove in from Charleston, South Carolina, and Aunt Carolyn, Moms only sister drove from Philadelphia, Pennsylvania. Everyone was cautioned to maintain their composure when in my presence because an emotional outbreak of a distraught state would make me cry. Tears would flow down the side of my face, even though my eyelids were taped shut. The sound of a familiar voice caused my body to respond in numerous ways; my eyes would flutter, tears would roll down the side of my face, or my blood pressure would increase. During the evening my goddaughter Melvina and cousin Felicia finally arrived from New Jersey and attempted to see me but visitation was denied by the I.C.U. nurse. The hospital staff wanted to obtain permission from Juan or my mom before anyone was permitted to visit me. My family was in another area of the hospital dining when this occurred. Melvina was persistent and refused to take no for an answer stating that she was my daughter and Felicia was my first cousin. The nurse didn't budge even though they had driven all the way from New Jersey to see me. The family finally returned to the waiting area from eating and Mom took them aside to prepare them before they saw me. They were asked to be strong and to try and maintain their composure. Mom explained to them that they almost lost me and that doctors had to consider several options to save my life. She told them that I wasn't going to look the same but all of the prepping was ineffective once they actually laid eyes on me. They cried hysterically. To them I was messed up. The sight of all the tubes and machines set off alarms in their minds that announced the worst. I wasn't going to make it. My swollen body looked like it was inflated with helium, and the cuts and devices were more than they could tolerate seeing. Although Mom tried to warn them, they could not be comforted, and were eventually escorted out of the area. It was worst than what they had expected to see. As they returned to the waiting room it took several minutes for them to regroup. They decided that before they departed Greenville, S.C. they were going to leave gifts. Melvina left behind, a teddy bear, balloons and a card, and Felicia left an angel figurine that remains in my bedroom to this very day.

On February 3rd family members continued to pray

and believe God for my healing as they spent the majority of the day between the I.C.U. waiting area and the hotel room. Jawane and Jazzmen visited me daily along with their father.

From the very second the children laid eyes on me, they both believed that I was going to make it. The disfigurations they saw did not interfere with their conviction. To them Mommy was a warrior at heart. The fact that I was still in the fight convinced Jawane that I was going to be victorious. He allowed his mind to recapture me training at Hillside Dojo with mostly men. Besides, Stephanie, Professor Miles daughter, there were no other females in the class. The mere fact that I didn't pass away at the accident scene spoke volumes to them. They figured that my injuries would not be able to end my life. They knew that I was going to fight until there was no fight left in me. Fighting is what I was good at. What they observed didn't matter. Jazzmen always believed that I was going to walk again; the broken bones meant nothing to her.

Then they came to Him, bringing a paralytic who was carried by four men. And when they could not come near Him because of the crowd they uncovered the roof where He was. So when they had broken through, they let down the bed on which the paralytic was lying. When Jesus saw their faith, He said to the paralytic, "Son, your sins are forgiven you." (NKJV) Mark 2:3-5 Which is easier, to say to the paralytic, 'Your sins are forgiven you,' or to say, 'Arise, take up your bed and walk'? (NKJV) Mark 2:9

My children handled seeing me in that condition extremely well for their age. Jawane thought of me as strong, pure hearted, and courageous. Jazzmen hoped I stayed tough, intelligent and hilarious.That combination in their eyes was a recipe that cooked up survival. God granted my children amazing strength to endure their current circumstances. Jawane repeated his gesture daily by gently rubbing my hand as he spoke, "Mommy, its going to be ok, its Jawane, I'm here, I love you mommy, I'm here". He was eleven years old at the time of the accident and his sister was eight. Whenever Jawane left my presence he wept like a child that kept falling off of his bike again and again. Jazzmen comforted her older brother and she rarely showed emotions during that time. She became who I am in the face of adversity. Always appearing strong, composed, and equipped to tackle any dilemma. Beneath what may have been mistaken for a nonchalant appearance, rested faith, love and strength. In the midst of everything that was going on, she remained eight at heart. She indulged herself with all of the ice cream that she could eat and continued to behave bratty as she annoyed her big brother. Juan continued to do all he could to make sure that they were content. Jawane caught a break from the reality of the situation by spending time in the arcade and playing basketball every chance he got. I returned to the Operating Room for my second surgery 48hrs later on February 4th, 2003.

During surgery I lost 450cc's of blood as doctors continued to repair my pelvic and sacral fracture. The external fixator was tightened on the area to realign my pelvic. My right foot sustained an open wound fracture causing me to lose fifty percent of my anklebone. The talar body was missing completely, but the talar head remained. The posterior tibial artery was still intact but it was not functioning. This is the artery that carries blood from the leg to the plantar surface of the foot. Also, the posterior tibial nerve in that same foot was significantly damage. My right foot suffered a calcaneus injury and doctor's were still considering amputation rather than additional surgeries. The external fixator was reapplied to my right foot with pins drilled into the tibia. My left hind foot was crushed severely, as the plantar area suffered an open wound injury and my toes were broken as well. The left foot was placed in a splint before I was taken to recovery. A few hours later I returned to the Intensive Care Unit for further observation.

My soul, wait silently for God alone, for my expectation is from Him. He only is my rock and my salvation; He is my defense; I shall not be moved. (NKJV) Psalm 62:5, 6

Wayne and the girls received the news that my surgery was successful before they departed the hospital. It was time for them to return to Georgia to make arrangements for Arty's Memorial Service. The drive home was full of apprehension and anxiety. None of them ever imagined what life would be like without her. Riding in the car without her in tow marked the first challenge of the lengthy journey ahead for them. The Memorial service was taking place on February 6th, Ashley's 12th birthday. I can't imagine and was afraid to ask what goes through the mind of a twelve year old girl who attends her Mothers home going service on her birthday. What should have been a day of festivity and tears of joy became one of grief and tears of sorrow. Returning to the house on Oliver Drive stirred up a lot of memories. It was the place that they saw her for the last time. The morning she departed the house became symbolic to the day she separated from this life. Wayne and Sophia were up to see her off having no idea that it was their final farewell as Ashley remained in bed asleep.

I sought the LORD, and he answered me; he delivered me from all my fears. (NKJV) Psalms 34:4

Pie arrived in Greenville with Debra Kennedy from her church, Bethel Outreach and Deliverance Ministries. She received the news that I was out of surgery and in recovery. She decided to check into the hotel and see how T.C. was holding up. He was discharged prior to their arrival and back at the hotel resting with his broken leg in a cast. When she arrived at his room he was really upset and could barely speak. A pool of tears filled his eyes, as he drowned in his own sorrows. Pie felt the energy that consumed him and she became overcome with empathy toward him, knowing that it was physically and emotionally stressful on him. She tried to comfort him as best she could before departing for the hospital. When she arrived at the hospital she was surprised to see a host of family and friends flooding the waiting room area. Pastor Jeannie, Mom's long time close friend and many unfamiliar faces stood out to her. She was overwhelmed by the show of support and sacrifice everyone had made to be with the family in Greenville, South Carolina. Mom returned to the waiting room where the rest of the family waited anxiously and greeted Pie and Debra. Pie was eager to see me, but mom informed her that it would be a minute because the nurses were in the process of returning me to the room. The nurses alerted the family when it was okay to go in and visit me, so Mom escorted Pie to my bedside and when she saw me she was speechless. She stood over me and stared while her eyes traveled the space where I rested upon the bed. She thought to herself, "Good Lord it's a lot of machines", as she followed the tube to the one in my throat. She observed the gash on my forehead; the sunken impression gave the opinion that it was hit pretty hard. She wondered why my eyelids were taped shut because my eyes continued to flutter as her and mom conversed. I was covered with sterile foam gauze while an external fixator rested on my midsection and right foot. Tubes were everywhere. Pie knew it was going to take a miracle to restore me to a place of normality.

He sent His word and healed them, and delivered them from their destructions (NKJV) Psalm 107:20

The nurse entered and Pie asked her what injury Arty died from, she responded that it was a skull fracture. After seeing me like that, she assumed that Arty had multiple injuries as well. They prayed over me before returning to the waiting area where family and friends were congregating.

And the prayer of faith will save the sick, and the Lord will raise him up. And if he has committed sins, he will be forgiven. (NKJV) James 5:15

Doctors informed the family that additional surgeries were needed to correct the disfiguration in my skeletal, muscular, and nervous system. Thank God that I was surrounded by an army of born again believers that believed in the power of prayer. The family continued to pray and believe God for the miraculous and formed prayer chains around the clock with people we knew locally and afar for my miracle.

Confess your trespasses to one another, and pray

for one another, that you may be healed. The effective, fervent prayer of a righteous man avails much. (NKJV) James 5:16

On Wednesday morning February 5th, Mom and Robin were planning to depart South Carolina to attend Arty's Memorial Service in Georgia. My other siblings, T.C. and Pie traveled back home to New Jersey to await Arty's funeral service. Dad remained in New Jersey the entire time, but stayed busy greeting family and friends and making preparation for the funeral service until Wayne arrived. Everyone from the neighborhood was very supportive and helped him get through the ordeal. Keith had made his way home from Massachusetts to be by his side and they kept everyone abreast of my condition. Dad held up well given the circumstance although losing a daughter suddenly was very painful for him. Sudden or unexpected death was nothing new to my father and his two brothers, James and Robert. They had lost their baby sister Lucille when she was only eight years old to a drowning accident. A few years later they lost their oldest sister Geraldine to tuberculosis, she was nineteen. Their father was fifty two when he died of cancer and their mother was thirty eight when she died suddenly from an asthma attack. When my father reached the age of twenty, he had lost his parents and both sisters.

Family and friends continued to show their support and arrive in Greenville, South Carolina, to be with the family. Elder Edward Burse worked with me at the Prison and his presence alone was appreciated and needed to assist Juan in enduring the lengthy journey that was before him. It was snowing in New Jersey as Edward boarded his flight out of Newark International Airport. He had no idea that Barbara Rodgers, and Elder Doretha Sims from Cathedral International in Perth Amboy, New Jersey were on the same flight. They were in ministry at the church I attended, but always went beyond the call of duty to help someone else. The weather conditions were severe as they lifted off in the blizzard. After they departed remaining flights were canceled due to inclement weather. God's favor was with them allowing them the grace to lift off before the airport shut down. Edward traveled hundreds of miles with a pillow in tow that had Mark 9:23 engraved on it.

Jesus said to him, "If you can believe, all things are possible to him who believes." (NKJV) Mark 9:23

I was surrounded by true saints who were orchestrated by God to be in my presence during that time that believed in the True and Living God and the power of agreement.

"Again I say to you that if two of you agree on earth concerning anything that they ask, it will be done for them by My Father in heaven. For where two or three are gathered together in My name, I am there in the midst of them."(NKJV) Matthew 18:19, 20

Ebony my god sister from Greensboro, North Carolina, arrived on that same day. After greeting the family Mom escorted Auntie Barbara, Elder Sims, and Ebony to my bedside before she departed for Georgia. Their presence made her feel more at ease about leaving since I was still comatose. She was happy that Juan and the children would have someone there with them while they were gone. As they approached my bedside the supernatural occurred because according to medicine I shouldn't have been able to see or hear them, but I did. I could not respond but for a brief moment, I captured a blurred vision of Auntie Barbara's red suit, Elder Sims leopard blouse, and streams of tears rolling down Ebony's face. I heard Auntie Barbara's voice as she spoke, "Cheryl, its Auntie Barbara. I'm here with

Aunt Doretha, and Ebony". She continued talking while everything in me tried to announce that her words were not falling on deaf ears. The next thing I recall was Elder Sims voice; "Cheryl, its Aunt Doretha, we just want to pray with you" as she began to anoint my body with blessed oil.

Is anyone among you sick? Let him call for the elders of the church, and let them pray over him, anointing him with oil in the name of the Lord. (NKJV) James 5:14

Ebony tried to get her words out between the sobs but was too emotional to speak. I don't know if it was an out of body experience or not, but all I know is that I saw them and I heard what they were saying to me.

For I consider that the sufferings of this present time are not worthy to be compared with the glory which shall be revealed in us. (NKJV) Romans 8:18

February 6th arrived and I was still hooked up to a respirator awaiting my miracle. Juan and the children spent a good portion of their day at the hospital. Edward departed for New Jersey, but Auntie Barbara, Doretha, and Ebony remained with Juan and the children. My condition continued to fluctuate from day to day and began to worsen. On February 7th, a significant amount of swelling was down, but I had to return to the Operating Room for my third surgery. I developed an infection in my blood and a deep hematoma was found on my left leg. The clotted veins were removed and tied off and my midfoot was pinned to keep it stabilized. Pins were placed in the left foot from the first toe into the hind foot to hold the forefoot together. The ankle was manipulated back into position between the subtalar joint that's between the ankle and calcaneus's. It was then pinned across the ankle into the tibia to allow my crushed heel to reform. Reconstruction of my left foot was performed while the right foot was only cleaned thoroughly, and the dressing was changed. The doctors planned to reconstruct that foot at a later time although amputation was still being considered. My body tolerated the surgery fairly well, and I was returned to the I.C.U. for further treatment. Even though I was unaware of their presence it never deterred Juan and the children from visiting me multiple times a day. They were happy to see me and felt that their being there was making a difference. Jawane continued to believe that if I continued to get surgeries I would continue to get better. Each time Jawane was at my bedside he gently rubbed my hand as he spoke, "Mommy, its going to be ok, its Jawane, I'm here, I love you mommy, I'm here".Auntie Barbara and Elder Sims presence at the hospital allowed Juan a chance to rest and regroup. The children played video games to ease their minds, and were taken to the mall and movies to break up the monotony. They continued to remain positive as my body rested and recovered from three surgeries in five days. Juan continued to keep family and co-workers back in New Jersey abreast of my situation. Fellow co-workers at East Jersey State Prison were very supportive and generous by calling consistently, and sending donations. They made sure that Juan and the children were comfortable and free of any financial burdens tied with being away from home. Still the greatest gift was the prayers sent my way.

February 9th arrived and only Juan remained with our children in Greenville, South Carolina, with me. The thought of departing before I was better was not an option for them. As long as I remained in the condition I was in they were not going anywhere. Getting through each day was their greatest challenge after spending long hours by my bedside in the I.C.U. They continued to hope for the best looking for an improvement in my condition, but I remained threatened with mortality the longer my body stayed connected to machines and not functioning on its own. Four days had passed since mom whispered in my ear, "Look up and live doll. God said, Look up and live" and my spirit began to gradually drift to the other side. I was missing my daily dose of spiritual food and was slowly slipping away. The doctors continued to pump sedative drugs into my veins that allowed my body time to rest and repair, but my organs were on a course of their own and started to fail.

Arty's funeral service was on Feb 11th in Trenton, New Jersey, at Grace Cathedral Church as snow blanketed the ground outside. The weather conditions made it difficult for T.C. to commute easily to the funeral on crutches with his leg in a cast. The pain was excruciating and penetrated deep down into the marrow of his bones. The truth of the moment drained all of his strength making it almost impossible to push pass the pain he felt. He became very upset and discouraged as he dealt with the reality of what that day meant. He decided to stay home rather than struggling. He didn't feel like dealing with all of the pressure. The family received a call from his wife that he was having a rough time and planned not to attend the funeral because of his battle. Rashawn Glenn, his best friend from childhood was made aware of his decision to stay home and immediately made his way to T.C.'s house to check in on his friend. Mr. Juney Gant, a friend of the family from the old neighborhood along with four of T.C's co-workers from the Department of Human Services showed up as well. The men encouraged him to attend the funeral and carried him in his wheelchair through the snow, and drove him to the church. Most of the family was gathered at the house on Ward Avenue where Arty grew up. Keith reminisced on the many years she walked in and out of that door, but it broke his heart to know that she would never walk through those doors again. He remembered her smile that could light up a room and her infectious personality that was contagious. The Limousine arrived and drove the family to the church as a host of supporters and friends awaited their arrival. Not one seat remained vacant in the entire sanctuary as old classmates, co-workers, neighbors, teachers, family, and friends created an overflow in the room. Pastor JoAnn Wilson gave a touching eulogy that comforted the heart of everyone present. The casket was covered with beautiful floral sprays and a noticeable standing arrangement that resembled a bleeding heart. The front of the church was decorated with crafted signs that read, wife and daughter. Her spirit has returned to the Lord, but her memories will forever remain in the hearts of all that knew her. She was a loving wife, caring mother, special daughter, compassionate sister, kind niece, thoughtful cousin, helpful neighbor, considerate co-worker, and concerned friend. The grief left almost everyone she knew speechless as they bid farewell to a pleasant, humble, and sweet spirited person.

On the day of her funeral I underwent my fourth surgery. Doctors discussed with Juan the possibility of amputation as oppose to several more surgeries on my right foot. He strongly disagreed with the option of amputation, but the doctor explained that I had lost a good portion of my ankle bone. Juan expressed that it didn't matter and to do whatever was necessary to save it. The doctor remarked that the decision whether to amputate or not would be made during surgery because of the missing bone and severely damaged nerves and joints. Juan kindly explained to the doctors in these words, "Let me put it like this, if that woman wakes up and finds her foot cut off, she will come looking for the person responsible." During surgery I lost 650cc's of blood and was given a blood transfusion. The doctors manage to successfully save my foot by performing an ankle fusion, but my lungs were still not functioning on their own. I remained on life support with a lengthy journey of recovery ahead of me as I returned to the I.C.U.

It was the 12th of February, and my body was not responding as well as doctors had expected it to. I was still comatose and my organs began to malfunction. The doctors explained that my lungs would shut down within fifteen minutes of being disconnected from the respirator. My condition rapidly declined within the next forty eight hours as I developed a high fever. I was critical and threatened with mortality, and rushed to the Operating Room for exploratory surgery on February 14th.

Mom retuned to Greenville and discovered that I was rushed off to have another surgery. The news she received hit her harder than a boulder falling upon her head. She had just finished the draining task of traveling up and down the highways and burying her firstborn child. The doctors reported that internal bleeding is what caused the fever, but they were able to stop it. He than informed her of the unpleasant news to make a decision to end my life. I was going to be given another lung test once I recovered from my surgery. The doctors suggested that if it didn't go well, the family should strongly consider taking me off of life support. Mom's faith had been tested to the extreme. She was at wits end not knowing what to do next. Juan and the children were back at the hotel relaxing, because they knew I was in surgery from earlier that morning. Juan returned with our children to the hospital as Jazzmen observed that her grandmother was back. She eagerly approached and said, "Hi Grandma, can you take me to the mall? I want to buy my mom a purple gown and robe. I want her to see it when she wakes up, it's her favorite color, and it will make her happy."

And said to Him, "Do you hear what these are saying?" And Jesus said to them, "Yes. Have you never read, 'Out of the mouth of babes and nursing infants you have perfected praise'?"(NKJV) Matthew 21:16

Right away mom knew that the decision was not up to her, or either of the doctors. She believed that God used my daughter to deliver a message.

Who hath believed our message? and to whom is the arm of the Lord revealed?" (NKJV) Isaiah 53:1

For with God nothing will be impossible." (NKJV)
Luke 1:37

She returned to my bedside and whispered in my ears multiple times, "Look up and live, doll. God said, look up and live." A few hours later my mom took Jazzmen to the store to fulfill her request. Jazzmen bought me a purple gown and robe. When Mom returned from the store, she made her way to my bedside and repeated, "Look up and live, doll. God said, look up and live". She stood on that scripture and held fast to her faith as she returned to the hotel room to fast and pray. The next day the test of my lungs returned the same negative result, my lungs would quit functioning under less than fifteen minutes. The bad news did not discourage mom. She continued to whisper in my ear, "Look up and live, doll, God said, look up and live". Although I was oblivious to my external surrounding, my spirit leaped every time mom recited, "Look up and live". The professional advice was rejected and for the next forty eight hours my soul went on a journey to find its way back. Mom was two days into her fast when the phone rang during the wee hours of the morning. She was in her hotel room reading her bible when the hospital called. The nurse on the other end of the phone recited, "Mrs. Brown, there has been a change in your daughter's condition. We need you at the hospital right away". The nurse revealed no further information. During the drive over to the hospital mom was at peace as she uttered, "Lord, thy will be done." When she arrived the doctor was anxious and excited to share the news about the change in my condition. He explained that I was making slight responses, and my lung function increased to forty percent of breathing on their own. With the machine doing less of the work, he wanted permission to unhook me from the respirator. Mom agreed as everyone stood back and witnessed the miraculous show up.

The glory of the Lord shall be revealed, and all flesh shall see it together; For the mouth of the Lord has spoken. (NKJV) Isaiah 40:5

The Spirit of the Lord once again breathed the breath of life into my nostrils. From that point on into the early morning hours my lungs continued to strengthen, forty percent increased to fifty percent, fifty increased to sixty percent, and so on. I was disconnected from the artificial breathing device as my soul depended solely on the True and Living God, maker of Heaven and Earth. To God be the glory!

And the LORD God formed man of the dust of the ground, and breathed into his nostrils the breath of life; and man became a living being. (NKJV) Genesis 2:7

I am the Lord, that is My name; And My glory I will not give to another, Nor My praise to carved images. (NKJV) Isaiah 42:8

Later that day my children were excited to see me off of the respirator and anxiously awaited me to wake up. They spent the remainder of the day close by with high hopes of seeing their mommy opening her eyes. The change in my condition had them really pumped up they could barely sit still. Jazzmen bounced around like a ball in a pinball machine. Their expectations were high. They thought perhaps I would be able to respond to them as I did before the accident. The entire family received the good news about the improvement I was making and rejoiced. The doctors said that I would probably use an oxygen tank the rest of my life, but God had other plans.

For I know the thoughts that I think toward you, says the LORD, thoughts of peace and not of evil, to give you a future and a hope. (NKJV) Jeremiah 29:11

On Feb. 16, 2003 fourteen days and six surgeries later, I opened my eyes to my new reality. I was no longer the person I use to be before February 2nd. I was in a fight that I had never fought before, this time it was literally for my life. I laid in the bed and calmly stared at the ceiling before catching a glimpse of Jazzmen running around the room. I couldn't move as I tried to figure out what was resting on my stomach making me feel pinned down. My son Jawane was the first to notice me watching them before leaping out of his seat and declaring with glee, "Mommy's awoke!! Dad! Look! Mommies awoke!" Jazzmen's frail body came to an immediate halt before inching over to check it out. Juan stood up and stared in amazement with a smile on his face as Jazzmen received a lip sync message from me indicating, "I am going to tear your butt up!" They all laughed before Juan notified the nurse that I was awake. Within minutes nurses were standing over me trying to explain what happened, but it was all a blur to me. I wasn't able to fully process the information or capture a clear picture of my children before slipping back into heavy sedation. When I opened my eyes again the nurse was in the room injecting medication into my intravenous line. She observed me struggling to say something because I still could not speak. I repeatedly moved my lips to ask her, "Where is my sister, how is my sister?" The nurse exited the room to retrieve my mom alerting her of the question I was seeking answers to. When my mother arrived I was resting well. Mom approached my bedside and said, "Hi doll, how are you? Take it easy; don't try to do too much." I then asked her the same question by only moving my lips, "Where is Arty, where is my sister?" Her reply was that she was in heaven. The news upset me; I didn't think she was the one that should have died. I turned away as the warm tears hit the side of my face and closed my eyes not wanting to open them again anytime soon. The very next day I asked the same question over again and responded as if I was hearing the news for the first time. My head injury caused short term memory loss and the medication I was given helped to erase what I was going through while I was in the hospital. Later that evening when Juan and the children arrived I motioned for a pen and paper to write my question out. I remember it taking all of my strength just to hold the pen and try to write. My mind was thinking one thing, but what showed up on the paper was all together different. It looked like a toddler had gotten hold of the pen and paper and was trying to write something. There were lines, circles, and unrecognizable marks, as Jazzmen broke out in a hysterical laugh at what was on the paper. I became frustrated before I finally gave up trying to ask, where my sister was. I continued to believe that she was in another room at the hospital or released. The doctors shared with Juan and my mother that I may continue to suffer temporary short term memory loss. The tracheotomy puncture was covered with gauze as a small tube protruded out of my throat area and was suctioned numerous times a day. I wanted to cough but I couldn't. Any attempt I made to cough, gave me the feeling of choking to death. It was very uncomfortable and painful at the same time because any amount of movement caused excruciating pain throughout my body. I was in the toughest fight of my life and it felt like I was losing the battle. Once I was able to get my mind to focus, the true fight was on I was determined to stay alive and conquer my life altering condition. Nothing or no one was going to get in my way, or hinder my progress.

It was approaching the end of February, and Juan and the children were out to pick up their laundry that he dropped off at the local Laundromat. The owner saw them earlier that month doing laundry and noticed the out of state license plates. She inquired as to what brought them to the area, and after hearing about my situation she offered free drop off service for the duration of their time in Greenville. The favor of God followed them wherever they went. My children's faces were becoming a regular at the local restaurants. They were provided with coupons to receive discounts on their next visit or ate for free. Not a single day passed that they didn't come by the hospital to visit with me. One particular night I could not fall asleep. The nurse gave me a sleeping pill as the pain wrecked my body. I was still restless and suffering from insomnia. I would drift off and wake up often like a newborn baby. I kept having a dream that I was flying and my sister Arty kept showing up in the dream. I continued to ask where she was, and how she was. Mom continued to tell me that she was in heaven. I was beginning to understand a little more each day that I had been in a bad accident, but no one mentioned or spoke to me about T.C. or Arty's condition. I continued to have the same dream and wake up in a cold sweat as the days ahead became very difficult for me. The pain was excruciating I was hungry and tired of being in the hospital. Mom announced to me that she was going to be leaving to take care of some business back home, but would be returning in two weeks. My dear friend

Carol Maggi from New Jersey was due to arrive before Mom's departure, and was going to remain until mom returned. Juan and the children were preparing to leave in order for the children to get back in school. It was a little difficult for me knowing that they would soon depart, because they had become my strength to carry on, and fight.

Fight the good fight of faith, lay hold on eternal life, to which you were also called and have confessed the good confession in the presence of many witnesses. 1Timothy 6:12 (NKJV)

Regardless of how I was feeling, I had to get my mind together for my upcoming surgery. The great thing about having my trachea tube removed is that the children had a chance to hear me speak before they left. It also would allow me to be able to talk to them over the phone while they were gone. The doctor entered my room with my daytime nurse Margarita, as Juan and the children watched. He removed the tube and replaced it with a metal plate and gauze. Whenever I wanted to say something, I had to press against the opening and speak. It seemed that when my voice came back so did my sense of humor. Before leaving the room the doctor asked me to try and say something. I pressed against my throat and moved my lips as though I was trying to speak, but I was only playing with them. The doctor and nurse looked at each other confused, as he stated, "this has never happened before". I pressed again, and said, "I'm only playing". A look of relief came over their faces and everyone in the room laughed. Five days had passed since I was off of life support and out of my coma being rolled into the operating room for another surgery. I remembered nothing about the surgeries prior to that one. This particular surgery was to perform a skin graft on the right foot that was fused where the open wound fracture had occurred. Skin was removed from my upper thigh and back area to cover the sight on that foot. Surgery went well and I continued to gradually improve. When I opened my eyes my friend Carol Maggi had arrived as she sat quietly in a chair listening to my grunts. The weight of the external fixator upon my abdomen continued to be unbearable and left me grunting of pain. Nurse Margirita would respond quickly and try to make me as comfortable as possible. Whatever she could do to make me feel better, she did it. It was time for Mom to depart, but before she left she reminded me to meditate on the Word of God daily and left me a bible she bought at the gift shop. The best part of my day was being entertained by Jawane and Jazzmen. It hurt like hell when they made me laugh, but felt good at the same time.

A merry heart does good, like medicine, but a broken spirit dries the bones. (NKJV) Proverbs 17:22

The reality of them leaving had me a little down although I tried not to show it. I had become use to them being around. Since the very first day I arrived at the hospital someone was there with me whether I knew it or not. It also concerned me about the long drive back to New Jersey that was before them. On February 28, 2003, my precious children and their father left my side and were going to be over eight hundred miles away. It upset me to know that I wasn't able to be there to pick them up from school, help with their homework, or cook dinner for them. With Juan returning to work at the prison and his part time security job, my family in New Jersey all chipped in to help out. It broke my heart to see them depart, but they had to get back to school. Thank God Principal Mark Broach allowed them the opportunity to make up all their missed work at Perkins Christian Institute. My children were in a private school system which made it possible for them to miss so many school days, and several snow days during that month rendered school closings in their favor. Mockers voiced their opinion regarding them missing so much school, unaware of the arrangements that were made with the principal.

It was good to see my friend Carol Maggi although I was surprised that she came from afar to see about me. I was very happy that she was there. Her presence made everyone in my family feel one hundred percent better that I was not alone. Carol was very attentive and fell right into her new role as my personal caregiver. She sat in my room from dawn to dusk watching me deal with the routine of a grueling day toward my recovery. It seemed as though my pelvis was getting an X-Ray every few days. I was turned on my side and then placed upon the cold hard film tray. It was unbearable and I prayed constantly for the external fixator upon my abdomen to be removed. If I wasn't getting an X-Ray, I was being stuck with a needle to have blood drawn. Every week my intravenous site was moved to a new spot on my arm or chest area to prevent infection. I hated being awakened at 6 a.m. in the morning to the nasty taste of ibuturol for my breathing treatment. It was a lot that I had to deal with, but all necessary on the road to my recovery. When March 1st arrived

I couldn't believe that I was still in the hospital with what felt like fifty pounds of iron on my torso. T.C.'s call made me feel better when he shared the news about my favorite fighter Roy Jones Jr. upcoming bout. I would have given anything to see it, but I later learned that he won. The news made me happy and no matter what my situation looked like I knew I was going to win my fight as well. Later that evening my children called. They arrived safely and were staying with my father. Dad was the only one with a schedule that gave him the freedom to attend to their every need. Carol was with me and her presence made the nurses respond quicker whenever I needed pain medication. She was such a trooper. She would spend the entire day at the hospital with me before returning to her hotel room to retire for the night. If I had a bad day where the pain got the best of me, she would remain in the room and sleep in the chair. She stood in proxy for Mom, and made sure that I wasn't mistreated. If I wasn't bathed by the time she arrived to my room in the morning, the nurses received a nice scorning. She never hesitated to help me herself. My life felt like it was regressing because what I use to be able to do for myself I no longer could. I was no different than an infant. I had to be bathed, fed, dressed, and helped with an everyday normal chore that we often take for granted. I would have given anything then just to be able to sit up on my own or use the bathroom without assistance. I was in a place that I never imagined I would be in. Everything that I once took for granted was stripped from me in minutes. To this very day, I'm still trying to recover the physical abilities that I lost as a result of the accident.

The doctors continued to share negative reports, but I was at a place that it didn't matter what they spoke. It's what I chose to believe. I wouldn't allow my mind to register those things that I didn't want to hear. If I didn't agree with it, I blocked it or immediately discarded contrary news from my memory bank. Days were tiring and long for Carol and me, but she was very helpful. I was also blessed with a great nursing staff for all shifts. It was only on their days off that I may have encountered a problem, although that was rare it did happen. Carol adored my nurse, Nurse John. We thought he was very pleasant and professional. He also had a great sense of humor and would stop at nothing to get me to laugh. Some days the pain was so intense that all I wanted to do is cry. Nurse John wouldn't stop until he got a smile out of me. Nurse Jeannie King was my favorite. She had such compassion, and reminded me of a grandmother.

She always had something sweet to say or would do something out of the ordinary for me. The weekend of March 8th was approaching and my sister Robin was coming on her birthday to visit me. Carol was going to leave once she arrived to visit her daughter in Atlanta. The weekend crept up quickly. Carol departed and Robin arrived bright and early in the morning. It was Robin's birthday weekend and she chose to spend it at the hospital all day in the room with me. I was glad that she came because up to that point I didn't exactly know what happened or how it happened. She asked me the question, "Cheryl, do you remember anything from the accident?" I told her the only thing I remembered was crawling into the back seat of the truck to sleep and that I kept having a vision of flying above the highway, over and over again. She exclaimed, "Oh my goodness, Cheryl you were flying, you were ejected!" Hearing her say that sent chills through my body and I didn't want to discuss anymore at that time. We were watching television when I heard a familiar voice as she came through the door singing... "I will do a new thing in you, I will do a new thing in you, whatever you ask for, whatever you pray for, I will not deny, saith the Lord, saith the Lord". It was Ebony, my god sister, and the sweet sound sent chills through me only this time in a good way. It was a pleasant surprise because I was not informed of her intentions to visit me. The two of them spent the weekend with me before departing on Sunday to return to their homes.

Jawane and Jazzmen continued to call me every evening around 6:30 p.m.. It became the time of day I looked forward to. The next day I was transferred to another room, and I wasn't happy about that. I was moved from a private room to one with a roommate. I couldn't wait for Mom to return to straighten that out. My roommate was an elderly woman that I assumed had a hip injury or hip replacement. She wasn't able to get in and out of the bed by herself, so she wore a diaper. I knew I grunted with pain, but my grunts didn't compare to what I heard penetrating from the other side of the partition. It seemed that she was in constant pain. She would grunt and cry out for the pain to stop. The nurses on that floor were lousy. They took entirely too long to bring pain medication and lacked compassion. It was only two days that I experienced this, but it seems like an eternity when the pain just wouldn't go away. The night shift nurse was pleasant, but the morning nurse was evil and mean. I would give her a look that meant more than any words could say. She gently and quickly did whatever she needed to do for me before torturing the elderly woman in the other bed. She would pull the partition before changing her and then screams would ring out. The nurse would try to talk over her screams and say, "Oh stop it, I'm not hurting you", but whatever was going on only occurred when she was attending to that woman. Once she was done the woman would moan and groan until she fell off to sleep. The next day the woman's family came in to visit and the nurse put on the biggest act in front of the family. After she left the room, I kindly let her children know that their mother was possibly being mistreated. Although I had a roommate it wasn't a very pleasant experience. I would have much rather been in a room by myself without anyone with me than what I experienced with that situation. I suppose it was my turn to keep someone else company. Later that day a private room opened up and I was wheeled to another floor. I was thankful for that. The task of being at the hospital without someone there with me around the clock was new to me.

The upcoming weekend, Wayne, Sophia and Ashley were due to arrive. Mom was still in New Jersey and wasn't expected back until the following week. The doctors ordered me to begin occupational and physical therapy. My therapist's name was Phil. He showed me how to use a sliding board to transfer myself from the bed into a chair. This particular chair was designed for paralyzed patients, but with the external fixator resting upon my abdomen it was suitable for my situation. The task left me exhausted and in severe pain, having to shift with bars across my body was very draining. After a dose of pain medication I would drift off to sleep. To me it made no sense to slide onto the chair and then back onto the bed fifteen minutes later. It was torture and so was receiving X-rays every few days to evaluate my pelvis healing progress. I was ready for Mom to return, but before I even had an opportunity to feel alone, God always had a ram in the bush.

Then Abraham lifted his eyes, and looked, and there behind him was a ram caught in a thicket by his horns: So Abraham went and took the ram, and offered him up for a burnt offering instead of his son. (NKJV)Genesis 22:13

Later that day after therapy and my nap, I observed a woman standing in the doorway staring at me with a big grin on her face. I starred at her and she stared at me before she laughed and said, "Hi Cheryl". I thought to myself who is this person that knows my name? She laughed again and said, "It's me Cheryl, Rita-beeta". RITA!! Rita Jett-Hopkins! At first I couldn't make out the face because she had all of her hair cut off and dyed blond. Shortly after she entered, Walter her husband came walking in the room. Rita was very special to me. We met at the Training Academy and worked together at the prison. Their visit brought me to tears. Rita and Walter sat with me until the late evening. After I ate dinner and received another dose of medication I began to fade out on them. They understood that I needed my rest and promised to visit me once I returned to New Jersey. The week was going by quickly and I managed to be doing just fine. On Thursday morning three of the surgeons walked into my room with their clipboards and I knew it wasn't going to be good news. They told me that my pelvis was healing crooked and that surgery would be necessary to correct it. It was believed that the weight of the external fixator and repeated shifting of my body caused my pelvis to shift. The surgery was scheduled for Friday morning, Wayne and the girls were due in on Saturday. If the surgery was successful my pelvis would be placed in a plate and the external fixator would be removed for good. To me that alone was good news. Once the doctors exited the room I called mom and told her about the surgery. She panicked and kept asking me, "How do you feel doll. Are you alright?" I told her I was fine and I was going to be okay so not to try and rush back. I told her to relax because I was tired of that contraption on my body and praying for it to come off. I remember praying that night," Lord, please don't let me wake up with this fixator on my pelvis. It's too heavy and I'm tired of it. In Jesus name Amen.

March 14th, marked my seventh surgery at that hospital. As I was rolled into surgery that morning I remember the brightest lights and a nurse that looked so mean. The surgeon made small talk, but I was out before I could even answer. My pelvis was healing crooked and it had to be jerked back evenly before a plate was placed over it and screwed in. I was awakened in the recovery room by a nurse. I remember being in the worst pain I had ever felt in my entire life. It was three times greater than labor pain. I reached down to touch my belly and the contraption was gone. I mumbled, "Thank you Jesus". That the external fixator was gone! I still had the one on my right leg and foot, but it was the one on my midsection that made it impossible to move on my own. I heard the nurse ask me what my pain level was on a scale of one thru ten, I moaned, ten. This was the first time that I was actually conscious after surgery and the pain was agonizing. Each time she asked me, I responded..."ten". I was in recovery over two hours and still in excruciating pain. I remember the look on her face as she told me "I can't give you anymore morphine, and I've given you all that I can." She looked like she wanted to cry with me, because I was crying like a baby. She just kept saying, "I'm sorry when you get back to the room the nurse will be able to give you something by mouth in a few hours".

When I arrived back at my room I remembered pleading and crying for pain medication. The pain was so intense. I cried, "It hurts, it hurts" is all I could get out. Through my tears I saw the mean looking nurse from the Operating Room standing over me. I didn't know what she was going to do as I cried and moaned for pain medication. She held my hand and asked me how I was doing. I just kept crying and begging for more medication. She asked me if it was alright to pray for me. I nodded yes, and she began to pray. Such a peace came over me and although the pain didn't leave I drifted off to sleep. Later that evening Nurse John entered the room on his rounds. It was his first night back from his days off and once he discovered I had surgery earlier that day he went to call the doctor. He had two percocets with him for my pain, but asked me to hold on because he had never seen me in pain like that before. Nurse John contacted the doctor to get permission to inject morphine into my I.V. line instead of me taking the pills by mouth that day. Morphine was pumped into my I.V. line allowing me some relief to get through the night. The next day the same doctors returned with good news! They explained what was done during surgery and informed me that in about two weeks I would be able to transfer to New Jersey since the external fixator was gone! I couldn't wait for the children to call that evening to share with them the good news. The surgery almost made me forget about Wayne and the girls visit. Up to that point, I was doing fine dealing with my sister's passing. I suppressed every emotion and pushed the thought of it to the back of my mind in order to get better. I tried not to concentrate on the truth that she was gone because I didn't want to fall into depression. Prior to them coming, I was a little apprehensive about seeing them. I think I was more concerned of what their response to me was going to be like. I didn't know if they were upset that they had lost their mother and I had survived. I didn't know what to expect. When they arrived I was still a little groggy from surgery the day before, but it was good to see them. Sophia was bubbly and talkative telling me everything that was going on. "Aunt Cheryl you know what?" … "Oh, and"…. I was amazed at the strength she displayed, and Ashley was being herself, reserved and quiet. She didn't say much just with a few giggles here and there. She was more interested in touring the hospital and going to the food court and gift shop then hanging around in a hospital room. Her big sister headed downstairs to take her to the gift shop and to get some food. Wayne stayed behind and shared the most amazing story with me. I was glad that he was able to talk about her, because I didn't know what to expect. He started by saying, "I know Artisse is in heaven, that is what's helping me get through all of this. When I returned from the funeral in New Jersey I was at the house. The girls had gone to bed and it started to rain. I went to bed too, and during the night I was abruptly awakened. It felt like Arty was right there in the room with me. The rain came down so hard it sounded like bricks were falling on the house. It felt like I was in a dream. I was lifted out of the bed and taken over to the window. I looked out and the rain fell so heavy and hard you could hardly see anything. When suddenly a whirlwind spun around collecting the rain off of the ground and what was falling, and shot up toward the heavens. It was a little peculiar so I went to lay back down. In the morning I couldn't figure out if I was dreaming or if it actually happened so I went over to the window again. I knew it had rained, but the ground looked dry, so I went out the front door to investigate further. As I walked to the end of the driveway I was bewildered at what I saw. Every house on the block, and the streets were saturated and wet. Not a drop of water was on my car, in the driveway, on the house, or grass, but it was wet everywhere else." Wayne said, he believed that it was Gods way of showing him that my sister was taken up before the accident even happened.

Then it happened, as they continued on and talked that suddenly a chariot of fire appeared with horses of fire, and separated the two of them and Elijah went up by a whirlwind into heaven. (NKJV) 2King 2:11

I was relieved after hearing that story and happy that they were doing ok. The girls returned to the room and this time Ashley opened up and started talking and laughing about what took place at the food court. I enjoyed them. Their visit made me forget all about the pain I was still in from surgery the day before and it gave me the strength to keep moving forward. Monday morning arrived and Phil walked in my room bubbly and loud. This time he was pushing a wheelchair instead of the long chair into my room. He retrieved my sliding board from out of my closet and showed me how to use it to get into the wheelchair by myself. I was discharged from Occupational Therapy, but received enough of it to regain some upper body strength. Not only did I think Phil was crazy, but I thought the Doctors had lost their minds as well. Hello people, I just had surgery on Friday! I sent Phil packing on this particular afternoon because my level of pain was still high and I was not in the mood to be moving around. I took some pain medication and rested a while. Phil returned later to conquer his quest but it did not go well. It was not easy sliding from a bed into a wheelchair because I still could not bear any weight on my legs. They were torturing me all over again! Once I was in the wheelchair I had to get use to sitting up straight after being flat on my back unable to bend for forty three days. I was sleeping on an air mattress and ingesting Coumadin to avoid getting blood clots. Needless to say, the physical therapy ordeal was my least favorite time of the day. Once I got the hang of it it wasn't so bad. I befriended a young lady on the same floor that had two broken legs from a car accident. We would park our wheelchairs in the hall and share stories about our life and experience in the hospital. Mom was still in New Jersey, but seeing her mother show up daily with her son reminded me of a mothers love.

Mom was on her way back to Greenville, and the moment she was on the floor I knew she was back. I turned my head and watched the door waiting for her to stroll in at any second. She came carrying a beautiful floral arrangement, and Melvina followed her, with a look of relief on her face. Mom had cards and trinkets from everywhere and began to decorate my room. It looked fabulous. The flowers she brought must have triggered a floral effect. Later that day flowers arrived from my favorite Lieuntetant at work, Daniel Murray. Before the week was out, Cathedral International, my church family sent me flowers and well wishes. After that bunch, Officer G. Williams Jr. had three dozen of roses delivered in red, pink and yellow the next day. Cards from family and friends filled one side of the room wall and the window was filled to capacity with all of the flowers and trinkets. Even the janitorial service lady gave me an angel. This trip for Melvina was better than the first. This time I knew she was there and it also gave her the opportunity to see the progress I was making. I remained in disbelief that I was still in the hospital. The thought of going home soon gave me some relief that at least that part of the journey would be over. Melvina didn't stay very long before taking the train back to New Jersey, and to my surprise Tammie and Curtis Gooding arrived from New Jersey to visit for a short stay. Tammie attempted to catch me up with all of the jailhouse drama before I politely shushed her from sharing any negative stories with me. Mom and Curtis departed the room and returned to their separate hotel rooms to allow Tammie and I time to spend together. Only once during my stay while mom was gone did I have the opportunity to leave the floor and see the hospital. I got in my wheelchair and Tammie pushed me up and down the hallways. We went to the food court and once I returned to the room I was exhausted. Rather than returning to the hotel with Curtis, she preferred to sleep in the room on the chair during the night to get the most out of her visit. The weekend arrived and The Gooding's prepared to depart leaving behind trinkets and a very generous monetary gift.

I was glad that Mom was back because my new found friend on the floor that I use to sit with was being discharged. Mom had the opportunity to meet her before she left. Approximately one week after she departed the therapist shared a newspaper article with me that she was deceased apparently from an undetected blood clot. The news frightened me and mom noticed that it had and she told me not to worry about what happened because it would not be my testimony.

A thousand may fall at your side, and ten thousand at your right hand but it shall not come near you (NKJV) Psalm 91:7, 8

Everyone that came into my circumference during that season was God sent. Two of the hospital Chaplin's would visit with me often with a powerful prayer and a scripture. They always took a minute to sit and converse with me. The local churches were diligent with routine visits of missionaries going from room to room to pray for the patients or share some good cheer. Venice was a young lady from the area that knew my family in Charleston, South Carolina. Venice was present from day one and continued to be supportive. She became like the big sister I had lost. She was very sweet and considerate, and took time out of her busy schedule to visit me often. Dorothy Manigult, a local Pastor was sisters with one of my mom's church members back home. She opened up her home to the family and sat with me on many days.

Mom and I were in my room watching television one day as Dr. Jeray, Dr. Kalar, Dr. Broderich, Dr. Goetz, Dr. Williams, Dr. Moore and Dr. Taylor walked in the room with individual clipboards in their hands. They greeted us before standing shoulder to shoulder as they flipped through the papers on their clipboards. One spoke at a time and then would ask another if he concurred. The doctors enlightened us about my progress, but also the seriousness of my injuries. They went on to explain as they stood at the foot of my bed that I would never walk again. I believe my response to the announcement left them baffled. I think they were expecting me to cry or yell, but not to defy what they had just said. After they shared that news, I simply said, "Yes, I will, I will walk again". One of the doctors almost became belligerent as he used medical terms to once again share that because of my multiple injures I would never walk again. He explained that my legs, ankles, foot, pelvis, and the fusion holding my foot in position were severe. Again I repeated, "Yes I will. None of that matters. Is that all?" They looked at one another as Dr. Kalar smiled and said, "I believe you will walk again" and Dr. Jeray agreed with him. Once they exit the room mom walked over to me and asked, "Doll, how do you feel about what the doctors said?" I told her what they said didn't matter. It's what God say's that matters and as long as I believe I was going to walk again, I was going to walk again.

Jesus said to him "If you can believe, all things are possible to him who believe" (NKJV) Mark 9:23

She said to me well I agree with you as she touched my leg and prayed the Word of God to seal our agreement.

Again I say to you that if two of you agree on earth concerning anything that they ask, it will be done for them by My Father in heaven. (NKJV) Matthew 18:19

Juan and the children were due to come in that weekend. I tried to convince them not to take that long drive because the hospital coordinator was making arrangements for me to fly home on March 25th. 2003.

My family from Charleston came to visit me on March 22nd. Connie, Gwen, Beverly, Caroline, Sandra, Preston, Kirby and Chubby all drove down to see me. During their visit I received another surprise as my co-worker Officer Mack stopped by to visit on his return trip to New Jersey from vacation. While I recovered and regained my strength I was able to speak more with family and friends on the phone. I received calls from Officer G. Williams Jr., Myra Abney, Sylvia Britt, and Vincent Welch. My cousin Karla Brown would call and awaken my spirit with her powerful prayers that carried an anointing straight through the phone lines. I was excited and ready to travel home. Tuesday morning couldn't arrive fast enough. When the 25th of March, arrived mom and I were bidding farewell to the hospital staff waiting for the okay to leave. We waited, and waited and waited. Staff and doctors continued to stop by to wish us a safe travel and say so-long. It was approximately 1 p.m. when the hospital coordinator came to my room to share some unfortunate news. She informed us that the flight was rescheduled for Monday April 1st, because the Medi-plane experienced engine problems and had to land in Maryland. I was thankful that we were not on the plane, but disappointed at the same time because I was ready to get home and see my children. We were also informed of the restrictions that needed to be fulfilled before my departure. I needed special equipment for my recovery and it had to be in place before I was discharged. On the list was a caregiver, therapist, an orthopedic, air mattress bed with a trapeze bar, commode, sliding board, wheelchair, and a wheelchair ramp had to be installed. Otherwise I was going to be sent to a rehabilitation hospital in Philadelphia, Pennsylvania. Although Philadelphia was much closer than Greenville, South Carolina I just wanted to be home. Everyone was waiting for me to arrive, but instead of me being driven up they received a phone call that I had to wait another week. After I gave Juan the news that I wasn't leaving until the following Tuesday, April 1st, 2003 he surprised me on Thursday March 27th, 2003 with the children. Mom made her way home once more to order the supplies and fulfill the demands attached to my discharge orders. My mom left on Friday and promised to send my sister Pie back to fly out with me on April 1st. Saturday evening as Juan was sitting in the hospital room with me, his brother Andre called to tell him that their father had passed and he needed to get back to New Jersey right away. The children hung out with me the rest of the day in the room so Juan could go back to the hotel to grieve and rest up. They departed at midnight so they could arrive in New Jersey by morning. Two months had passed since the accident and I prayed that it was the last trip they would have to make to South Carolina to see about me. Once everyone was gone I started to not feel so good. I wasn't lonely or depressed; I was nauseous and running a temperature. I tried to sleep it off because I didn't want anything to interfere with me leaving out on Tuesday. No matter how much rest I tried to get or water I ingested, the symptoms remained. Pie arrived first thing Monday morning just as the shifts were changing. The nurse was in the room taking my vitals and I was still running a fever. When they checked it again my temperature had increased. I was given medication to break the fever, but it was not working. The nurse didn't know what was going on. By 5:30 p.m. on March 31st, 2003 two of my doctors and the hospital coordinator came to the room to inform me that I would not be able to leave in the morning due to my fever. I was informed that I needed to be fever free for twenty four hours before I could be released. I called mom to share the unfortunate news with her as she began to pray over the phone, "Take your hands off of her body, she don't belong to you, spirit of infirmity, I bind you in Jesus name! I command you in the name of Jesus to loose your hold, release her now! In Jesus name". As she was praying chills went throughout my body. She softly spoke, "Get some rest Doll, you are coming home. The next flight won't be canceled." I hung up the phone with mom as dinner was coming through the door. I ate and was making myself comfortable when my entire body became soaked. I was sweating profusely. I asked Pie to get me another gown and some fresh linen because I believed my temperature had broken.

When I pulled the covers down I noticed a huge blood stain in the center of my gown. Pie called the nurse. She checked me out, cleaned me up, and called for the doctor. It was discovered that the incision from my surgery two weeks earlier had opened up. The site was infected and the cause of my fever. After mom prayed that prayer the fever broke and the infection in my blood seeped out of my body through the only opening it could find. What a God! Rather than being on a plane flying back to New Jersey. I was returning to the Operating Room for my 8th surgery at Greenville Memorial Hospital.

And we know that all things work together for good to those who love God, to those who are the called according to His purpose. (NKJV)Romans 8:28

On April 1st, I was being wheeled back into the Operating room rather than out the door. In the morning the staff was shocked to see me returning to the Operating room. This was the day I was supposed to be leaving. The nurse in the O.R. area sang, "Let me touch you, and see if you are real," by Kirk Franklin, as she began my IV. I said, "Oh, that's my song." She replied, "I remember the day you came in, sweetie you were in bad shape, God has brought you from a mighty long way, as I look at you now I know He is real. You are so blessed" umm, umm, umm. Thank God it was another successful surgery. I realized that I didn't have to come back from sedation once they put me under.

The pain was nothing like the surgery before and I had a new date to go home, April 9th. Pie contacted mom about my surgery and the new date. When I spoke to my mom the next day she was going to fly out the day before my departure. Pie left on Thursday and the thought of being left alone was no longer an issue for me because every time my family or friends were away God made sure he sent me a guardian angel.

"I will not leave you orphans, I will come to you."(NKJV) John 14:18

Two of the therapist's that assisted Phil came to get me on their lunch break and took me on a grand tour of the hospital. Greenville Memorial Hospital is a state of the art facility. It put me in the mind of a mini mall with a variety of gift shops, and a large food court. It contained several eateries' to suit any taste bud: Subway, Chik-fa-'li, Chinese Food, Baskin Robbins, and the Cafeteria to name a few. A glass elevator carried you from one floor to the next. The lobby area on the main floor had a grand piano in the center floor surrounded by plush chairs and plenty of silk trees and paintings. The chapel was beautifully architected and you didn't have to leave the grounds to do any banking because a credit union was right there inside with nice clothing stores.I spent my last week in Greenville rolling around the hospital visiting patients and praying for them as I shared my testimony. Mom arrived on April 8, 2003 and repacked all of my belongings. Finally, I was going to be leaving Greenville Memorial Hospital. The next morning I was excited. Two doctors, my nurse, and the hospital coordinator arrived at my room with my discharge papers. I couldn't believe that I was really leaving this time. The paramedics arrived at my room to transport me to the airport by ambulance. This particular morning it seemed like everyone was out of their rooms or away from their work station to say, "So- long", have a safe trip", or that word I had grown to despise, "goodbye". They lined up from one end of the hallway to the other to say goodbye. The distance from the hospital to the airport was less than thirty minutes and the flight home felt quicker than that. When I arrived at Mercer County

Airport, I was so happy to be back in New Jersey. It was snow on the ground and cold but that didn't change the elation I had. I spent the day before sitting outside in seventy five degree weather only to return to snow. Paramedics met us on the airport grounds and drove us to mom's house. Just as I was settling in to prepare for the journey ahead of me there was a knock at the door. I thought it was my children, but this time it was my DAD.

Chapter 6
The Journey

The LORD will perfect that which concerns me Your mercy, O LORD, endures forever; Do not forsake the works of Your hands. (NKJV) Psalms 138:8

It felt good to finally be back at home in Trenton, New Jersey. What began as a road trip turned into a journey through time that cannot be retracted or erased. I saw the gates of heaven as my sister transitioned to the other side. I rested in the wings of angels, the ministering spirits as I was delivered up out of harms way. I experienced wrecking pain in my body that was so intense and continuous like the promise of hell is certain to be. I wasn't there, Thank God, but the unremitting pain made me feel like I was going through hell on earth. Life has a way of propelling us into situations that we would have never imagined being thrust into. I didn't know that I would be able to endure spending sixty-six days in the hospital, but by the grace of God I did. Some people don't make it through one surgery, let alone twelve in a lifetime and be blessed to write about it. I suffered numerous broken bones and three internal injuries, but looking at my life today no one would have ever known what I have been through.

My brethren, count it all joy when you fall into various trials, knowing that the testing of your faith produces patience. But let patience have its perfect work, that you may be perfect and complete, lacking nothing. (NKJV) James 1:2-4

In the midst of all the discomfort and suffering, God was nigh.

The LORD is near to all who call upon Him, to all who call upon Him in truth. He will fulfill the desire of those who fear Him; He also will hear their cry and save them. (NKJV) Psalm 145:18, 19

Three months in one place can seem like a long time, but it went by rather quickly. I was still incapacitated when I arrived home. Mom had the dining room turned into a replica of my hospital room. A large hospital bed equipped with an air mattress, trapeze bar and rails rested downstairs in the dining room floor. My wheelchair, sliding board, and commode were strategically positioned for easy access in the night hours. Mom continued to be a full time nurse, chef, therapist, and grandma around the clock. The children were with me at moms, and in the morning Dad would pick them up and take them to school.

Three times a week a private nurse was assigned to be dispatched to the house to draw my blood because I was sent home on Coumadin. The medication is a blood thinner that prevents blood clots from forming. I recall the first day the nurse arrived at the house. She was an elderly woman of a Portugal descent.

Once she opened her mouth her assignment with me was over. I was sitting in my wheelchair having breakfast when she arrived. Mom had just finished bathing me and changing the linen on the bed. The doorbell rang; Mom answered the door, and greeted her before returning to the kitchen. The first mistake she made was resting upon my bed because I was highly prone to infection. I didn't want outside germs from her other patients transferred to me. Strike one! She introduced herself and the next words to come out of her mouth were, "How are you doing since they scraped you up off of the concrete?" Wow! Everything inside of me shattered. Her words struck me like someone walked up to me and slapped me in my face for no apparent reason at all. I recovered quickly from the unexpected blow, but Mom heard her and immediately left the kitchen. Strike two! Mom asked her, "What did you just say to my daughter"? She said "I was asking her how she was doing". She proceeded in her attempt to draw my blood without gloves on or washing her hands. Goodbye! Mom politely asked her to leave and reported her to the nursing company.

Throughout the day Mom kept asking me if I was o.k. because I looked down in spirits. I didn't appreciate the comment. It wasn't her comment that sent me on an emotional decline; it was a glimpse of my sister's obituary that caught my eye earlier that day. Arty's death was becoming more real to me as the days passed, but I wasn't ready to deal with it. The following week April 18, 2003 on her birthday I began to process everything that had taken place. In Greenville, I was focused on getting better, receiving treatment, surgeries, therapy, and visitors that I didn't get a chance to miss her. It was on her birthday that it hit me the hardest, she was gone. I quickly gathered myself and rejected the very thought of her passing so it wouldn't get me down. Everything was going well and rather smoothly with the children and I at Mom's house until an electrical problem occurred. The electrician was called to diagnosis the situation and discovered that several rooms needed to be rewired including the one that I was in. Mom wasted no time having me transferred across town to my brother T.C.'s house until the work was complete. My mom feared that if an electrical fire occurred, it would be difficult to get me out of the house in time.

I made the trip across town which was supposed to be temporary, but lasted six long months. Dad, T.C. and Keith packed up my equipment and placed it on the pick-up truck to be carried across town. I was carried out in my wheelchair later that day and rolled into the Winnebago. It was the only vehicle large enough for me to travel across town and remain in my wheelchair.

Jawane and Jazzmen were excited to be around their cousins and felt very relaxed in the beginning. The position I was in was uncomfortable and at times very embarrassing for me. I have always been a very independent person, or the one that was providing the help to someone else. It was quite difficult being in a place that required full time assistance; No one knew how I felt. I needed help bathing, getting dress, and shifting from my wheelchair into the bed, among other things. I received an abundance of support from my family and friends, but I always felt like I was a burden to them. It was a devastating feeling not being able to do the things that I use to do for myself. I felt helpless like a cripple and it almost broke my spirit. The majority of my time was spent sitting in the recliner watching television or I would catch up on some reading. "The Purpose Driven Life", was hot off the press during this time and given to me by a friend for my reading pleasure. I've always been a very studious individual that loved to read and research, so my recovery became the prime time for me to really "get it in".

Doctor appointments were frequent and I was transported by Ambulance on a gurney and babysat by paramedics to every doctor's visit. Mom and Juan would attend the appointments with me as they followed behind in the car. I remember the looks on people's faces as I was rolled in and as I was rolled out. They stopped and they stared! Never being inconspicuous or at least trying to be, people literally stopped whatever they were doing to watch me. Little children were curious about the apparatus attached to my right leg as they pointed and questioned their parents who shushed them. The looks became annoying, but I tried not to let it bother me because people are going to be people. During the day one of my parents stayed at T.C.'s house to assist me throughout the day with all of my needs. A caregiver arrived early in the morning, at 6:30 a.m. five days a week. The caregivers hours were extremely too early for me. I wasn't hungry at that time and very drowsy from ingesting Oxycodone to manage my pain throughout the night. The majority of my tasks were not accomplished in the small window during her visit, and handled by one of my parents during the day.

The end of the school year approached, which meant that my parents could take a break and the children would be with me during the day. Jawane and Jazzmen were use to luxurious vacations during the summer, but because of my condition it was impossible to fulfill. I was scheduled for surgery in July to have the external fixator removed. The morning of the surgery Mom was with me. I was released the next day and returned to my brother's house. I continued to take my pain medication as prescribed although it didn't help much with the pain. I continued because it helped me to rest and became more of a tranquilizer than a pain killer. After attending my post-op appointment, a physical therapist was sent to the house to begin helping me regain strength in my legs. The day Bill, the therapist showed up, the children clowned how he favored the man from the Geico car insurance commercial. Bill was tall and slim with a wild curly afro. He was good at his job. The therapist worked with me for three months and the furthest I got was hopping on one leg using a walker for a short distance.

The summer months with the children home during the day caused tempers to flair and frustration to rise. They were at each others throat constantly fighting and bickering. The ambiance in the house was full of discord and strife. It was time for my children and I to go, but where? I was still wheelchair bound, unable to work, and not fully recovered. Most Sundays, I was driven to church in Dads Winnebago. When we arrived at Cathedral International Church, Brother Quinton Fields, one of the security guards at the church, greeted me on my arrival and pushed me through the church doors. Once church service ended, Brother Fields would roll me out and into the mobile home.

The situation at my brothers' house had become too

much for the children and I, so we all had a weekend getaway. They spent the weekend with their dad and I stayed at Auntie Barbara's house in Perth Amboy. On September 7th 2003, after church service as I sat in her kitchen having dinner everything hit me hard. The realization of my present situation had taken its toll. I was still in a wheelchair. I had nowhere to live, my children were unhappy, and I felt like I couldn't do anything about it. It broke my heart. I broke down and began to cry. I didn't know how to explain to Auntie Barbara, and Geneva Evans what was going on it was too emotionally painful. I tried to get it all out, but I was distressed. I didn't want to return to my brother's house, and I told them that I wanted my own place. We joined together and prayed a prayer of agreement. I asked God specifically to bless me with a three bedroom apartment by October 1st, 2003. I took into consideration what God had just brought me through. I knew an apartment wasn't a hard thing for Him. I returned to my brother's home.

On Monday after sharing my desire with my mom, we began apartment hunting. We went to several places during the month putting in applications. On September 26, I was shocked that none of the places

I applied to called me back, but I held fast to my faith. It was all I had.

So the Lord said, "If you have faith as a mustard seed, you can say to this Mulberry Tree, Be pulled up by the see and be planted in the sea, and it would obey you. (NKJV) Luke 17:6

On Monday September 29, 2003 two days from my hearts desire, I began making phone calls only to find out that every single unit was rented to someone else. I was devastated. I cried silently and in the midst of me crying my niece yelled out for me to pick up the phone because I had a call. I quickly wiped my tears away and answered the call thinking it was about an apartment. Instead it was Elder Doretha Sims. She said, "Hello Cheryl, it's Aunt Doretha, Auntie Barbara told me that you and the children were going to be moving", when I heard those words it was like I heard it from heaven. Aunt Doretha prayed for me before we hung up the phone. She had no idea that her call was on time. I shared with Mom the news about all of the places being rented to someone else, but that didn't matter because on Oct 1, I was going to be in my own place. It was September 30, 2003 and I still believed God had a place for me to live. I was considered unemployed to the landlords and I had no chance of finding housing if I was going to operate in the natural. Mom and I went to see several places I found in the morning newspaper. I disqualified most of the rentals based on the neighborhoods or porch steps it took just to get to the front door. Mom suggested leaving the Trenton area and looking in Ewing Township. We were driving into one of the complexes when I noticed that the sign advertised one and two bedroom apartments. I told her that it was a waste of our time because I needed three bedrooms. Mom suggested we look at them since we were already there. I refused to get out of the car so mom went to the office and retrieved the keys to the model apartment. I stayed in the car until she returned with her report. Mom came back and explained that it could work, but it was a two bedroom apartment. I told her no, I asked for three bedrooms and that is what I was going to get. Mom returned the key to the office, but before she could pull off Cindy the manager came running out of the office building yielding her to wait. She said, "I have one more apartment I want you to look at. We rent it to our college students because it has a den that can be used as a third bedroom". Cindy went on to suggest that the builders made a mistake when they were constructing it; because it was the only one out there like that; they called it a two bedroom with a den and the rent was slightly higher. Mom went to look at the apartment and returned excited saying, "Doll, its perfect. It's wide enough for your wheelchair and there are three bedrooms, but the only challenge is that you will have to climb a flight of steps before you enter the apartment. What do you think?" I was satisfied just hearing that the den had a door and was large enough to be used as a third bedroom. I submitted an application that morning. I was less than twenty-four hours away from my miracle. Cindy gave me a list of numbers I would need to call if the application was approved.

Mom and I drove to Keasbey, New Jersey where my P.O. Box was located to pick up my mail. As I was going through the pile I noticed mail from Aflac that looked like a check. Aflac was paying a portion of my salary, but that payment was not due for another week. When I opened the envelope it was a check for ten thousand dollars! I had no idea that the rider I had purchased paid per limb for every bone I fractured in the car accident. While we were back in Trenton Cindy called to share that I was approved and could pick up my keys in the morning, October 1, 2003. God did it in twenty-four days. The God of Elijah showed up and showed off! I called Public Service Electric and Gas (PSE&G) company to have the services transferred over into my name. I called Auntie Barbara and Geneva to share the good news that October 1st, just as we prayed was the day I would be moving into my apartment.

The children were excited when I shared the good news with them and we spent the rest of the day furniture shopping with our ten thousand dollar blessing! It was hard to sleep that night because I was overwhelmed with gratitude unto God for answering my prayer just as I had requested.

Delight yourself also in the Lord, and He shall give you the desires of your heart, Commit your way to the Lord, Trust also in Him, and He shall bring it to pass. (NKJV) Psalm 37:4, 5

October 1st, 2003, arrived and I was heading to my new home at 9 a.m. to sign my lease, pay the security deposit rent, and pick up my key. When I came out of the office Auntie Barbara, Geneva, and Harriett Barnes were parked in front of the door waiting to celebrate what the Lord had done.

This was the Lord's doing: it is marvelous in our eyes. This is the day the Lord has made will rejoice and be glad in it. (NKJV) Psalm 118:23, 24

Auntie Barbara and the ladies had the back of her pick-up truck packed to capacity with groceries and toiletries. Mom helped me out of the car and thru the door as I scooted up the staircase to see my new place for the first time. Great job God! He did a great job. My soul was overjoyed as I contemplated how He knew me before that day ever arrived.

For I know the thoughts that I think toward you, says the Lord, thoughts of peace and not of evil, to give you a future and a hope. (NKJV) Jeremiah 29:11

I thought about what Cindy had shared about the builders making an error when they were constructing the place. What an error was in mans eyes was pre-ordained by God. God had me and my children in mind and knew what we would need and the exact time we would need it. Auntie Barbara, Geneva and Harriett began to unload the groceries and supplies that they blessed us with. Every cupboard was packed to capacity. They filled the freezer with meats and the refrigerator was stocked as well. The linen closet ran out of space as they piled in toilet paper, toothpaste, air fresheners, cleaners, lotion, and everything that I would possibly need. The God of Elijah came through in the eleventh hour, but He was on time. Dad picked up my children from school and they were happy to be in their own home. We waited for the furniture to be delivered the delivery men showed up with the children's beds only. I had become use to sleeping in a recliner since I wasn't able to lay completely flat. Dad delivered the recliner to me, but I would have slept sitting up in a wheelchair to avoid going back to anyone's house. I was in the last days of having a caregiver and therapist come to the home. I was in the stage of regaining my independence and it felt good.

Home therapy soon stopped and I was picked up three times a week and driven to Lawrenceville Rehabilitation Center for therapy. I was learning how to use the walker and build up my endurance to walking further and longer. I also learned how to drive using hand controls since I was unable to use my right foot as a normal driver would due to my ankle fusion. October in our new home was a breeze and Jazzmen turned out to be quite a helpful little nurse around the house. I tithed on the money I received, paid the rent for two months, purchased furniture, and paid towards the children's tuition.

It was a Sunday morning the 23rd of November, 2003, and I had attended every service that month except this one. It was very cold out and Mom suggested that I stay in. Jawane was at his football game with my brother T.C. and Jazzmen slept late. I wished I was at church as I thought about Bishop Donald Hilliard Jr's. sermon from the past two Sundays. He preached from a series "Pick up your bed and walk". I still had the fragments of that sermon in my spirit as I rolled around the apartment. I went into the living room to watch television, but couldn't find the remote control. I entered the doorway of Jawane's room and saw it at the other end of his dresser. My wheelchair was too wide to fit through the space so I went to get Jazzmen. She was sleeping soundly and I didn't want to disturb her. I rolled back to Jawane's room and locked the wheels on my wheelchair before attempting to stand. I figured that if I held on to the bed and dresser I could make it to the other end. I got up and put weight through my legs even though the doctors instructed me not to bear weight on the right side. When I got to the other end, I felt like an infant walking for the first time. I wanted to try it again. I grabbed the remote and sat on the bed to rest. Walking a short distance was exhausting, but I felt like I accomplished something. I sized up my chair and how I was going to turn around to get back into it. When I stood up, I noticed that I felt little to no pain so I let the dresser and bed go just to see if I could stand on my own legs. I did! I decided to let go and move my legs. I did it! I continued to practice in that small space back and forth. I was so excited. I went to wake up Jazzmen to show her what The God of Elijah had done. Jazzmen grinned, clapped, and turned over to go back to sleep. I couldn't wait for Jawane to return home from his game because Jawane knew how to get happy with someone else. Jawane also became animated when he was excited.

Oh magnify the Lord with me, and Let us exalt His name together. (NKJV) Psalm 34:3

Jawane returned home from his game as my brother T.C. and a few of the other players remained outside. When Jawane came up the stairs I asked him how the game went. I had purposely positioned an object to retrieve so he could see me walking again. Jawane stood at the top of the staircase telling me how the game was, but in the middle of him talking I rose up out of the wheelchair and walked over to the object. Jawane was startled and took off running down the steps yelling, "Taliel, Shaquin, Robert, my mom is walking! My mom is walking!" The boys jetted in the house, as T.C. followed. I was sitting back down in the wheelchair when my nephew Taleil said, "Aunt Cheryl what is Jawane talking about?" as the other boys watched. T.C. approached and said, "Cheryl, what's going on?" I grinned, rose again, and walked over to them as Jawane followed with my wheelchair. T.C. was in shock! He didn't move right away. He just stood with his eyes and mouth wide. Right away he called his wife and said, "Sabrina, this dag on girl is over here walking, yes, Cheryl, and I can't believe this either". The boys cheered and celebrated the goodness of God before their eyes. The God of Elijah was not done with me yet.

I continued going to rehab with braces on both legs as I learned how to drive using hand controls. The very first time I took the drivers test I passed using the hand controls. Receiving my license allowed me a greater independence to be able to drive myself around again. Only thing was, I no longer owned a car. My brother let me use his Ford Windstar which provided me with enough leg room to be comfortable or I rented a vehicle on the weekends to drive myself to church. I spent the year getting back to doing things for myself and living what man deems a normal life. Two thousand and four was a long tedious year for me. Although I was beginning to do things for myself, I still needed help with the smallest tasks like changing my linen, cleaning, or washing the laundry. My parents picked up our laundry weekly and grocery shopped for us. Life was challenging for the children because they became my full time caregivers. A case of role reversal was in full affect. I was able to drive them to the mall and other places, but my son had to help me in and out of the car, lift my wheelchair, and push me around. I was able to stand and walk short distances with the assistance of a walker, or three prong walking cane. I preferred being pushed in the wheelchair since I didn't get very far walking in the beginning of my transition back to becoming vertical. I was discharged from rehab because it was nothing further that could be done for me. I had reached my max based on my injuries. I had to force myself to do all of the exercises on my own if I wanted to be free of all the contraptions I had accumulated. My recovery was slow as I continued wearing a leg brace, special shoes, and attending many visits to the doctors office.

In April of 2005, my sister Pie wanted to take me on a vacation so we planned a trip to Jamaica. Two days before we were to leave the reservations were lost in the system even though the money had come out of our accounts. We ended up in Virginia Beach. The weather was crappy. It rained everyday and it was very cold. During our stay in Virginia, we had favor with God and with man. When we arrived at the hotel, Pie was helping me out of the car, as the manager stopped what he was doing and rushed over to help. The Manager told Pie to park in his assigned spot because it was closest to the door and gave us a free parking pass for the duration of our stay. Later that evening at dinner as we waited for the check, the manager came to the table and told us that dinner was on the hotel and offered us to dine free of charge during our stay. When Pie asked why it was free, he stated that our order was misplaced and had taken longer than normal to be delivered to our table. He observed that we never behaved unseemly or fussed. He simply said, "Your attitude and presence is warm and pleasant." It's a pleasure having you in our establishment."

When we returned home Expedia sent vouchers granting us four hundred dollars off of our next trip after the discrepancy with our Jamaica arrangements. Pie found a reasonable trip to Aruba that same day so we were finally going to get some sunshine after all. My bones were aching for the healing warmth of the sun rays. When we arrived in Aruba, the handicap accessible rooms that we requested were all occupied and we were upgraded to a spacious suite at no extra charge. During our stay at a fabulous resort, I met a lady from New Jersey that walked with a limp. I still had the brace on my legs and a cane to get around. The woman stared before approaching me to ask what was wrong. Initially I thought she wanted to exchange war stories, but what she shared turned out to be my blessing in disguise. Her name was Cynthia and she shared with me her story which involved a car accident with siblings as well. She too had lost a sibling from the accident and our injuries that related to broken bones were exactly the same. Cynthia's ankle was fused too, but she had on regular shoes and didn't walk with a cane. I asked her how she was able to wear regular sandals, and walk without any support. Cynthia admitted that in the beginning she had the same apparatus as well, but one day decided that she was going to walk without them. I was astonished not because of her story, but, because The Lord redirected our steps to allow me to see what He was about to do in my life. He allowed our reservations to become lost in cyber space in order for me to meet Cynthia. When I returned to New Jersey, I went on a three day consecration. I didn't want or need anything. I just desired to get closer to the Lord. Once I finished praying I heard the Holy Sprit say in a still small voice, "Unsnap the brace". I removed the brace and attempted to stand up and walk. I wasn't able to so I sat back down before I fell. I heard the instruction once again, "Unsnap the brace", I attempted once again, only to become disappointed and question myself if it was God's voice that I was hearing. I heard it once more, "Unsnap the brace"; I looked at the brace and realized that it snapped into the brackets made into my shoes. I unsnapped the brace from the shoe and placed the shoe on my feet and I have been walking without the brace ever since.

Throughout the years, The God of Elijah has continued to touch my body in a miraculous way. I learned how to drive with hand controls and I eventually weaned myself away from them. I was using my left foot to control the accelerator and brakes like other drivers use their right foot. The ankle fusion made it impossible at first to drive like a normal driver until one day as I was backing out of the driveway I was able to use my right foot without even trying. When I noticed that my right foot was on the accelerator, I tried to switch back to the left foot. I received a miracle in my driveway.

The Lord continued to transform my mind and my body followed suit.

The next thing God did was put a Woman of God in my life by the name of Belinda Benjamin. Belinda came to me one day and said, "The Lord told me to buy you a bike." Belinda had no idea that I had a plate over my pelvic area to keep it intact which makes it difficult to straddle. She delivered the bicycle to me one day with these instructions, "The Lord said to practice getting on and off". I then shared with her the revelation of my plate and difficulty of not only straddling, but balancing and stopping because of my ankle fusion. I followed the instructions, and within thirty days I was riding my bicycle up and down inclines with no problem.

One day as I was out shoe shopping I became frustrated because every shoe was touching the bone that protrudes at the bottom of my left foot. I continued trying on the flattest shoes with my special insoles, but nothing fit comfortably. In the night hour, I had a dream that I was walking straight in high heels and running in them as well. I thought to myself, who told me that I couldn't wear heels anymore. I returned to the shoe store and started trying on high heels. It was painful and frustrating because I could barely stand in them let alone take even one step. I regrouped and began to try on wedge heels instead of stilettos. You go God! He gave it to me in a dream and brought it to pass. Even as I lay in that hospital I would see myself walking in a vision. The Lord told me that he was going to heal me completely and He is not done with me yet.

But those who wait on the LORD Shall renew their strength; They shall mount up with wings like eagles, They shall run and not be weary, They shall walk and not faint. (NKJV) Isaiah 40:31

Chapter 7
Reflecting Back

All I have are memories we shared from growing up. We were a trio. If mom called out to one, she called out to the others as well. When the street lights came on we heard; Arty, Robin, and Cheryl lets go! Who would have ever thought that she would be the first to go, literally? I would imagine that it was hard for her being the first born. It had to be tough. My sister had no blueprint to follow. She was always the first to experience or try something for the first time. Arty was the ideal role model for any younger sibling. She was intelligent, pleasant, pretty, humble, and reserved. Her smile would light up a room wherever she went. We were all unique and distinct with our own personality traits. I guess I would be described as the rebel of the bunch. I was bold, courageous, always fighting and never afraid to try something new. I was the middle child and in my eyes it was a greater challenge trying to live up to or match the qualities of my older sister. Arty and I had a three year gap between us, but she and Robin were closer. T.C. and I had the same space between us and we hung tight. I was happy to finally be the older sibling over someone rather than trying to keep up. This time I made the blueprint for someone else to follow and I didn't make it easy. It was difficult being the third born, because Arty set the bar so high. She handled being the eldest rather well. She was poised and always seemed to be in control. At sixth grade graduation, she was Valedictorian of her class. For the next few years if you didn't exceed or match her accomplishment in Dads eyes then you did nothing notable of praise. While she made things look easy, I struggled to follow in the same footprints created for me. Arty brought home straight A's effortlessly. Gym was probably the only class I obtained a steady A in. I was a B student and sometimes C's. Growing up was challenging for me when she was placed in the gifted and talented class. She was the first to go off to junior high and high school. Robin the second born always had one of us in front of her and one of us behind her so she never experienced the solo state as Arty and I did.

I remember the day Arty was hit by a car. I didn't know what to expect when I received the news that she was taken to the hospital. She returned home with a cast and crutches. Although Robin and T.C. were around, I became her legs when she needed something. She had other surgeries that followed to correct the injury yet still she was left with a limp that forced her to walk on her forefoot. She was the first child to be injured or have a broken bone so I guess being the first to experience something wasn't all it was cooked up to be.

Arty had such a respectful nature about herself. She possessed a sweet humble spirit and was full of love. Everyone in the neighborhood admired her. She would go from stoop to stoop sitting and chatting with the senior citizens and when I asked her why she talked to them so much her reply was, *"No one remembers them when they get old."* Arty felt it was her obligation to make them feel loved and not lonely. Normally, mom and dad made us all go places together, but the weekend the fair was in town I was at grandma's house and Robin was on a date. Arty ended up getting into an altercation which resulted in her being jumped by several girls. Once The Ward Avenue girls; Robin, Tonya, Connie, Leshay, Etta, Merline, Kim, and I heard about the altercation, we wasted no time settling that score.

In 1984 Arty graduated from Trenton Central High School. This time she was graduating in the top one percent of her class and going off to attend Trenton State College. She was the first grandchild to go off to college and I remember grandma being so proud of her. Freshman and sophomore year flew by quickly; it was in her junior year that she met her husband Wayne Brown, the father of her two daughters, Sophia and Ashley. I thought it was funny that she was always going to be a Brown, and wondered how it felt to be marrying someone with the same last name. Arty became pregnant in her junior year, and exit college early to fulfill the duty of motherhood. When Sophia was born, Grandma was excited to help out, which allowed Arty the opportunity to return to college to receive her degree in Early Childhood Education. Sophia was two when their family relocated to Hawaii. Wayne and the family moved away in order for him to fulfill his new tour of duty after enlisting in the United States Army.

In 1988, Robin and I made our first visit to see our big

sister, niece, and brother in law. I was rather shocked, yet pleased to see her balancing being a wife, mother, and career woman. Their home was immaculate. Meals were delicious and Sophia didn't have a strand of hair out of place. Everyday Sophia was spotless from head to toe with the cutest outfits. This is not the same Arty I remembered growing up with. That person didn't like to clean up or cook. Academically, she was a scholar, but when it came to domestic affairs she was lazy. Marriage and motherhood changed that for her. I returned once more to Hawaii with Juan before Wayne's tour ended.

In 1991, The Brown's next tour was in Virginia which gave the family an opportunity to visit more frequently. While in Virginia a new addition was added to the Brown family, Ashley Kerrin!

The Brown's continue to move from base to base over the years before settling down in Georgia. The girls transitioned smoothly into the school system and became great athletes and honor students. Both played basketball and Sophia ran track. Athleticism must have come from their father Wayne because clearly Arty didn't have an athletic bone in her body. Arty's academics and artistic skills was a force to be reckoned with I suppose the girls gained their intelligence from her. Georgia appeared to be their final destination giving Arty the opportunity to further her education. "Ms. Arty" as she was known to the children began teaching in the Georgia School system. Students and parents loved her. Arty exercised such patience with the most challenging students that she became well known for her method of getting what society deems a problem child and turning them into a good student. Arty loved teaching and working with children, but not more than she loved the Lord or serving in her church. She connected with Free Chapel Worship Center, Pastor Jentezen Franklin, and worked in the children ministries. She also worked part-time for Wachovia Bank as a teller. Arty seized every opportunity to spread the gospel and evangelize wherever she went. She was faithful and committed to the Lord and to her church family. Our Mother is a Woman of God, so growing up in our household we were taught that worship was the foundation of our being, tithing was an act of obedience, reading the bible was our roadmap, and prayer and fasting released power to change any situation. If any home knew the power of prayer and fasting, it was our household on Ward Avenue in Trenton, New Jersey. Mom had no problem calling us in from playing to participate in family prayer.

The last time I saw Arty was the morning of completing her forty day fast. Arty sat peacefully with such a glory cloud around her. The atmosphere in the room was very eerie. I recall such peace being in the room, yet simultaneously it was an unusual feeling. I watched her sit calmly in front of the computer as I grabbed a bite to eat. I saw her physical body before me, but it was like I could see through her at the same time. There was a strong presence in the room releasing a force field that surrounded and protected her every move. No one spoke a word. Whatever was taking place was happening right before our eyes but we couldn't see it. It looked like she was deep in thought, but felt like she was between heaven and earth. Arty approached the door; she turned around and said, "Sophia, take care of Ashley", bye Wayne. Before departing Georgia we prayed in the driveway, *Our Father which art in heaven, Hallowed be thy name. Thy kingdom come, Thy will be done in earth, as it is in heaven...* I said "see ya" to Wayne and Sophia as I climbed in the back seat of the SUV to sleep as Arty sat quietly in the front passenger seat. When I awakened from my rest, Arty was gone. The End

Acknowledgements

Thank you Heavenly Father for the gift of life and allowing the Holy Spirit to bring this encounter back to my remembrance.

I am grateful to so many people that God orchestrated to be in my life for such a time as this. Thanks again, Mom and Dad. You have shown me unconditional love all of my life. Thank you for the encouragement and support throughout the years.

To all of my siblings, Thank you for going out of your way to make sure that I was comfortable. I appreciate your understanding when I was a thorn in the side. Thanks for your patience and going out of your way to make sure that I was comfortable, when I know you would have rather turned my wheelchair over.

To my family members, Auntie, Carolyn Patterson, Cousin Preston, Beverly, Allen, Sandra, Gwen, Carolyn, Connie, and the entire Snowden crew. Thank you for being there from beginning to end throughout my recovery.

To Juan Hooper, Thank you for stepping up to the plate when I needed it the most. Thank you for the excellent care you gave to our children when I was down. I appreciate you being firm with the doctors and refusing to allow them to amputate my leg. Thank you!

To my Cathedral International Church family, Perth Amboy, New Jersey, and Bishop Donald Hilliard Jr. Sr. Pastor: Thank you for the continuous prayers, cards, flowers, and financial support throughout my recovery.

To Bethel Outreach Deliverance Ministries, Trenton, New Jersey and Pastor JoAnn Wilson: Thank you for all of your help and the generosity shown to my family during a difficult time.

To Free Chapel Worship Center, Gainesville, Georgia, and Pastor Jentezen Franklin: Thank you for the kindness, love and care you extended to Sophia and Ashley after the loss of their mother.

A special thanks to Carol Maggi, my sister, my friend, and my nurse. Thank you for sacrificing your time and spending restless hours at the hospital by my bedside.

To Tammie Gooding, Thank you for being a loyal friend. You were my second half cheerleader. You cheered me on during the time I needed it the most. You helped me get over the final hurdle. Thanks for being there through the rough times.

To my Auntie Barbara, Thank you for the nourishing food that added strength to my body and soul, and loving me like a daughter.

To Elder Henry and Pinkie Rodgers, Thank you for praying me through and visiting even when I was unaware of your presence.

To Aunt Doretha, Thank you for loving me as a niece and touching heaven with your prayers.

To Edward Burse, Thank you for responding swiftly, and taking the time to travel many miles to see about me. I forgive you for never putting in my car radio.

To my favorite lieutenant Daniel Murray, Thank you so much for the beautiful flowers every week. They kept me smiling and eased my pain when I couldn't say a word. Thank you for being a true friend.

To Venice, Thank you for sitting countless hours by

my side and sharing your warm smile that brightened my day.

To Dorothy Manigault, Thank you for being a home away from home to my family and for the many hours you spent at my bedside.

To Carla Brown, Thank you for helping me see people through God's eyes.

To Vincent Welch, Thank you for being a friend that sticks closer than a brother.

To Belinda Benjamin," The Motivator" God used you to help birth this book into fruition. You are truly anointed. Don't ever stop "Saying Something".

To Jeuron Dove, Thank you for helping me during the early stages of this task.

To Janelle Spearman-Stout, my sister, my friend, and my confidant. I couldn't have done this without you. You came through when everyone else let me down. I Thank God for using you to keep this vision alive until it was complete. Thank you for believing in me. You are an incredible person.

A special thanks to PBA #105, Lymandia Allen, and a mighty prayer warrior, Mother McLeod. .

And last but not least...To the hospital staff and Surgeons at Greenville Memorial Hospital, and a special thanks to the on site paramedics and ambulance crew. Thank you for saving my life.

Thank you to anyone I may have left out that sent cards, flowers, said a prayer, visited or called me on the phone. Thank You, Thank You, Thank You!

In Remembrance

Of

My loving and dear sister, Artisse Elizabeth Brown

April 18, 1966 – February 2, 2003

Miss you Arty. R.I.P

Suspended in time

I remember the day, I was suspended in time.
Getting some rest was the only goal on my mind,
as I stretched out completely to rejuvenate the soul,
unaware of the test to come as
I was sent soaring toward the sun
my mind announced your flying,
all I could think of was, am I dying?
An angel gently placed me on the concrete
as bones splintered through my feet.
As I laid there on my back
I didn't know my pelvic was not intact.
I pushed and pulled but nothing happened
within seconds my lungs were collapsing.
No air was felt through my nose
as they struggled to get the tube down
but my airway had closed.
The work ceased after many attempts
before the call to the hospital was sent.
Suddenly, I lifted my arm across my chest
the work resumed without a rest.
Scissors were cutting off the scraps of clothes
as I drifted into a place no one knows.

Hooked up to a Respirator, with eight tubes in my
body
Long surgeries, lots of pain,
and intensive care following my name
I was comatose and broken bones were everywhere
internal injuries were present too,
was I going to make it?
Only God knew.
As day turned to night and night turned to day
family and friends continued to pray,
believing that God would make a way.
Sixteen days later I opened my eyes
and saw my children at my bedside
I tried to talk but had no speech
because they had done a trachectomony.
I drifted again into the deep
on this side I looked asleep.
I fought hard to hold on to life,
as the pain kept stabbing like a knife
February left, and march came in,
I remained the same when was it going to end
No strength, no change, no chance of going home.
It was 800 miles away, I felt so alone.
The calls, the cards, the beautiful flowers,
still nothing could erase the long long hours.
It was April, when the doctors came to talk,

saying never again will I walk.
I said not only will I walk but I will run,
wait and see the day will come
after sixty six days I was leaving floor three,
it was an awesome send off they had for me.
My bones I thought would never mend,
as the days progressed and they refused to bend
I was still rolling around in a wheelchair,
with not enough strength to even comb my own hair
External fixators drilled into my bones,
no weight bearing, why did I come home?
The walker, the cane, and the orthopedic shoes,
bone stimulator and more bad news
My journey has been quite a task
now this question I must ask
Of all the things I had already gone through
did it take this to draw me closer to you?
Everyday I place my feet on the floor,
the constant pain pounds on my door
I never gave up, thanks for your grace
that helped me to get to this place
I remember the day Heaven gave her a key
To spend her life in eternity
Since that day I stay on bending knee
It's what it will take to complete this journey
Cheryl Simone